ECONOMICS FOR THE NON-ECONOMIST

I0474186

SERGEI SHISHKIN

DENVER, COLORADO

Economics for the Non-economist

Outskirts Press, Inc.
http://www.outskirtspress.com

ISBN: 978-1-4787-5480-0

Outskirts Press and the "OP" logo are trademarks belonging to Outskirts Press, Inc.

PRINTED IN THE UNITED STATES OF AMERICA

Table of Contents

Preface

Who needs such a book? No one! From the day we are born until sometime after we die, we play our part in economics—every day, every hour. We instinctively know about economics not because someone told us, but because we have had our own experience with it. So why should we waste our time and eyesight?

Because from time to time real-life questions arise—questions to which our knowledge and experience can give us no quick answers. Why, for example, do store prices increase while our income does not? How can we put aside a little more money? Where should we keep our modest nest egg? We can ask our friends, of course, but where is the guarantee that they really know what to do? Various experts expatiate in the media, and they may very well know what they are talking about. But if your friend is well read or the expert is very knowledgeable, his or her discussion of the matter is simply too difficult to follow, and you are not inclined to feel like a complete idiot. So this is your book. It is a book for those who want to be able to carry on a conversation about economics in serious company, but more importantly, it is a book for those who want to widen their horizons and to better understand the world they live in.

Money and Prices

We should begin, of course, not with money, but with "goods". In terms of economics, goods are products that we set aside for later use or exchange for other items; they are items that are not used by the person who made them immediately after they have been produced. Once we have "surpluses" (items that are not immediately consumed) that we want to exchange for something we need or want, money comes into play. Money is very simply the means by which we can easily exchange one set of surpluses for another.

And yet it is more interesting to begin with money. Somehow money has more magnetic qualities.

As human beings, we know everything there is to know about money. Almost. As the noted group ABBA confirmed in the last century, "Money, money, money. Always sunny in the rich man's world. "

Usually governments print money, but money precedes the appearance of the modern state. Primitive tribes have had money from time immemorial or, more precisely, from the time when different tribes, pursuing a variety of occupations (hunting, fishing, gathering), began to exchange the fruits of their labors among themselves. This means that money served a definite purpose that was recognized by the whole society independent of its organization, whether it was a primitive tribe or the city of London.

Money has taken many forms: shells, furs, flint axes, beads, pigs, bulls, and so forth. Some theoreticians have divided money into "real" and "nonreal". Nonreal money includes those things that can be used apart from their value as a means of exchange, such as a flint ax. To the category of real money belong those things that have no value apart from their designation as a means of savings and exchange. Here, for example, we find dollar bills or paper euros; hardly anyone is going to use them as scraps of notepaper. You can, of course, find money that, due to monetary reform or changes in state governance, no longer functions as a means of exchange. If it has artistic value, you can frame it and hang it on the wall.

This theoretical analysis, however, is debatable. Take gold, for example. Its aesthetic, chemical, and physical properties give it both technical and decorative value. And, even though it is virtually excluded from state systems of payment, no one is going to reject gold as a valuable means of acquiring wealth.

There is a direct connection between money and power; the volume of economic and literary writing on the subject is such that it is not worth even beginning to cite the sources. This connection is diabolical. Money bestows power, and power begets money. Any government takes care to ensure that it has the power to print or mint money. Within their borders, the authorities will forcefully squelch the competitive printing or minting of money that has a legal and common acceptance as means of payment. The act of counterfeiting official currency always carried severe penalties in legal codes.

Now let's suppose that you are an absolute ruler of a state, and on your orders all your subjects are required to accept the money you issue (coins or paper bills) to pay for their goods and services. So that they cannot refuse, you declare that all government taxes and fees will be payable in this same currency. You use it to buy things and pay your court and staff. Except for funds you might set aside, all this currency enters the marketplace and pays for the goods and services produced by your subjects—by the farmers, the craftspeople, the weavers, the tailors, the hairdressers, the artists, the poets, and everyone else. The volume of goods and services, however, is limited by the ability and willingness of your subjects to produce and sell them. For this reason, no matter how much money you might print or mint, it can buy only the products that are available in the market. We can illustrate this as follows:

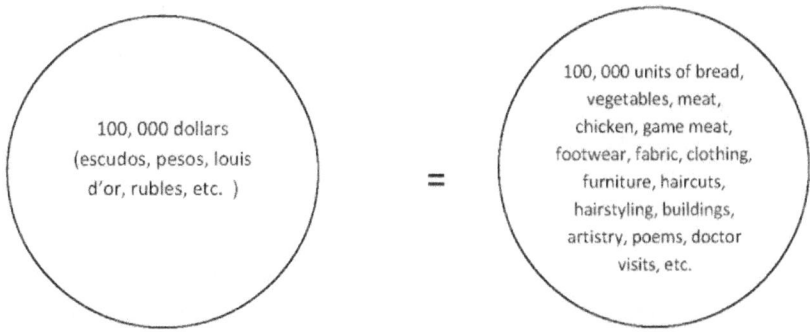

100, 000 dollars
(escudos, pesos, louis
d'or, rubles, etc.)

=

100, 000 units of bread,
vegetables, meat,
chicken, game meat,
footwear, fabric, clothing,
furniture, haircuts,
hairstyling, buildings,
artistry, poems, doctor
visits, etc.

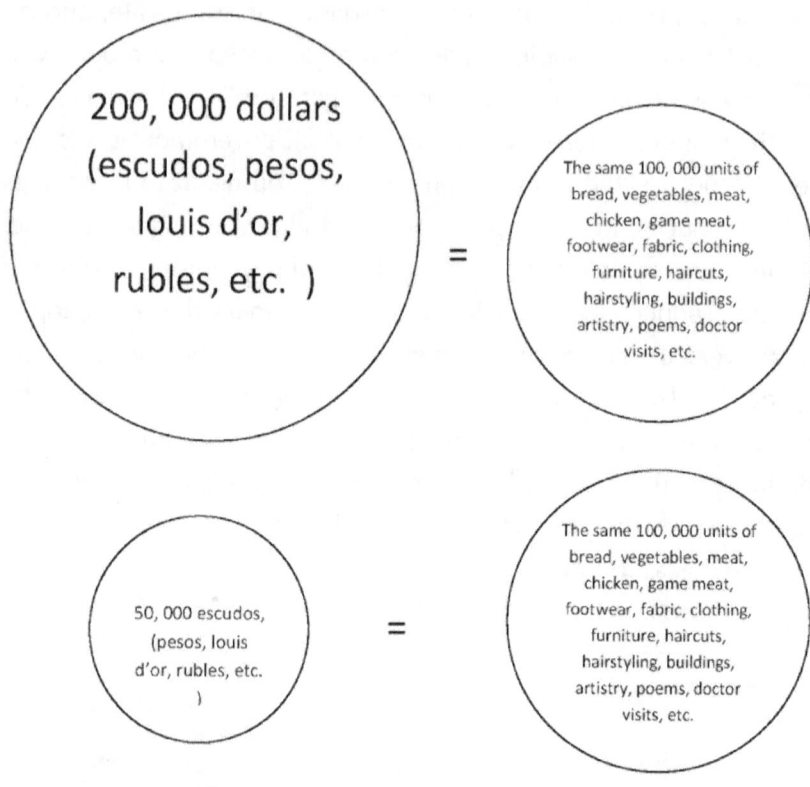

200, 000 dollars (escudos, pesos, louis d'or, rubles, etc.)

=

The same 100, 000 units of bread, vegetables, meat, chicken, game meat, footwear, fabric, clothing, furniture, haircuts, hairstyling, buildings, artistry, poems, doctor visits, etc.

50, 000 escudos, (pesos, louis d'or, rubles, etc.)

=

The same 100, 000 units of bread, vegetables, meat, chicken, game meat, footwear, fabric, clothing, furniture, haircuts, hairstyling, buildings, artistry, poems, doctor visits, etc.

Part of the money you have issued will not enter the marketplace. Some of the people to whom you have given money (your court, guards, armed forces, and civil servants) will put some of it aside in a rainy-day fund (for kids' education, daughters' weddings, building a summer cottage, etc.). Because some money from prior savings will also be entering the market, we will not consider this as a separate pool of funds. Likewise, some quantity of goods and services will be sold without requiring a cash payment. The sellers or suppliers give it away on trust, wishing to consolidate their business or attract new clientele. Some part of their trust will, they hope, be repaid later in hard cash. For the time being, we are not going to consider these details. We must remember, however, that one bill or one coin will circulate in the market and pay for goods or services more than once. You pay your tailor for sewing a dress, the tailor uses this money to buy wine, the wine seller pays for a haircut with the same coin or bill, and so forth.

Although it is rather difficult to describe how this happens, the market is very sensitive to the amount of money that is added to it. Let's imagine that there is a baker who every day has fresh bread and rolls for sale. Today, everything sold out sooner than it did yesterday. At the same time, the fancier breads and pastries were sold before the basic breads because the customers had received more money from whomever issued it. The next day, the baker mixes more dough and bakes a few more bagels and cupcakes, and starts raising prices to take advantage of the rising demand. But he is confronted by two problems: first, there are physical limits to the expansion of his production, and secondly, the customers start to complain and go to the competition.

More money would also be spent on things once considered extravagant or luxurious (paintings, sculpture, odes, serenades), and the artists and sculptors could bring more money into the market for commodities they need. Our baker would wrestle with the problems of building another bakery and hiring more workers. In short, the market regulates the expansion of production just as it regulates the growth of prices. This would seem to be a good thing. The quantity of marketed goods and services would increase, and with the same amount of money in circulation, prices should fall.

Things, however, are not that simple. As we saw, producers, sensing the growth in demand, tend to raise the prices for their commodities. The people to whom you pay wages will begin to complain about higher prices and ask for increases. But this is not so bad. What's worse is that when money trickles down to the lowest level in the chain of money flow (usually those who produce raw materials and food), the quantity of money diminishes. So, for the people in these categories, it is a bit less than for other levels. Prices increase but the income of those who are the last to receive the money does not keep pace. Because of this, the people take up arms and begin to destroy the shops and granaries, and you, as the ruler, are left with the option of increasing the size of your army or police (with a corresponding additional expenditure) or buying up the staples and distributing them to the poor, which once again requires additional funds. In short, putting additional money into circulation is a delicate and highly political affair.

As the ruler, you can put any figure (denomination) on coins or banknotes you put into circulation. You can make the coins or banknotes pretty to look at. What you can't do is change the proportion between the money you have already issued for circulation and the volume of goods and services that exists in the marketplace. And this proportion is expressed in prices. The winners from the increase in the quantity of money in circulation are those who were first to get them—as a rule, those closest to power, the civil service, and armed forces. But these advantages are fleeting. The market reacts to this by increasing prices, which soon eats up any increase in salary.

We can express the definition of the quantity of money in circulation by a simple formula that looks like this:

> The necessary quantity of money equals the value of all goods and services available for sale minus what is sold on credit plus the amount of credit paid off minus the increase in net savings; the total should be divided by the velocity with which the currency units circulate.

There have been times in history when excessive money in the market or **inflation** reached irrational levels. After the First World War and the civil war of 1918–1922 in Russia, the ability to produce goods and services was decimated. Practically nothing was available for sale, and anyone who owned anything tried desperately to exchange it directly for other needed items. Yet it was impossible to stop printing of money. The army and civil servants had to be paid, and even though it was rapidly downsizing, the military was armed, dangerously ill-directed, and with some justification considered itself to have won new powers and to be worthy of corresponding compensation. Food rations, however, were considered the main compensation at the time, not financial reimbursement. The level of inflation was such that, in order to lower costs of issuing and circulating new money (the money had to be counted, transported and stored), every paper ruble issued by the government was equal to ten or a hundred thousand rubles that had been issued during the previous year. Coins were generally not minted since there was an insufficient quantity of the necessary metals. We find a very similar situation at the same time in Germany. Nevertheless, money continued to play one of its roles—the means of exchange—although in a very limited capacity. Its second function—the means of accumulation or savings—had failed completely since its value was eroding by the minute.

There is an interesting psychological aspect to the role of money. Apart from the intrinsic value of the metal from which it is minted, the value of the currency depends on the level of trust in the power that issued it. We will talk about this a little later. Here we need only to remember that money is necessary not only for the rulers who issue it, but for all those who participate in the circulation of goods and services; without currency, this circulation would be extremely difficult.

We must not forget about the cost of the material from which money is made. In the United States, the current cost of minting a one-cent or five-cent coin is more than the face value of the coin (the number stamped on it), but the government continues to issue these coins to maintain its reputation. In inflationary conditions, it may be beneficial to hoard coins and use them for their metal. This is exactly what happened with Russian coins in the 1990s when a number of neighboring states suddenly became exporters of base metals on the global market although they had no natural resources of these metals.

Besides internal reasons that limit the issuance of money, there are external forces that influence the process.

Let's suppose that a neighboring country produces a certain fancy product that your own state does not. That state's sovereign and his wife pay you an official visit, and your wife admires this particular item that she sees on her counterpart. Well, you know sooner or later (the sooner the better!) you are going to have to make an effort to purchase it. The currency in the neighboring state, however, is different from yours. What can you do? If you mint your currency from a material that is in general use (gold, platinum, silver), you can take it to the salesperson in the other state. He or she can then take it to a jewelry store and get local currency at a price that depends on the weight of the coinage and the content of valuable metal (assay).

But what if there were no jewelry stores available or if they already had more metal than they could handle? As commodities markets and states developed, so too did the institution of moneychangers. The moneychanger observed how many people were ready to buy the currency of another country and how many offered the domestic currency in exchange. From this basis, they established corresponding exchange rates for these currencies. With this in mind, we need to introduce a correction into our formula for the quantity of money needed in the marketplace. We must subtract the quantity of money that flows to other states and add the amount that comes in from beyond our borders. In parallel with this, we must add the goods that arrive from other countries (**imports**) and deduct the goods that are sold outside the borders by your vendors (**exports**). Since money and goods are closely linked with each other in the market for goods and services, then roughly speaking, exports and imports equal the quantity of money coming in or leaving the country. But this is not always the case.

You can see that if the equilibrium of our formula is upset by an increase in the left side of the equation (the volume of money in circulation), the result will be inflation as expressed by an increase in prices. If, for some reason, the right side of the equation starts to outweigh the left (that is, the volume of goods and services increase but consumers are not willing or able to spend more money to buy them), prices fall. Does this ever happen? Oh, yes.

Take, for example, the market in a small, sleepy village or town. In strawberry or cherry season, prices will fall as the produce arrives in the shops. And take seasonal sales in stores, which have a very noticeable psychological impact on the buyers, although sometimes new ticket prices are set higher (including their placement on the price tags) than the initial prices, which then become the "lowered" prices. Naturally, this is pure highway robbery but psychologically it works well. Or take what happened in the USA in 1973 at the height of another in a series of Middle East crises. At that time, the oil-producing countries of that region curtailed the sale of oil to the United States and other countries that supported Israel. So the available quantity of the everyday commodity—gasoline—without which the country would be paralyzed, dropped sharply. The price at the gas pump immediately doubled and then tripled, and still there were half-mile-long lines at the gas stations. What happened was that the quantity of goods decreased, but the amount of money in circulation remained the same.

You can often hear the complaint: "Prices in stores are increasing, not by the day but by the hour. And yet the official data on inflation does not show this. What's going on? Another falsehood for public consumption!?" It's more likely that the statistics are simply manipulated. In stores, you would encounter only a limited set of goods and services. But statistically speaking, the cost of living encompasses many other services that you are not using at any given time. Let's say that the cost of housing falls. Insofar as housing costs are a significant part of the expenses of the population as a whole, the inflation statistics show a decline, even as prices tags in the shops show the opposite trend.

Apart from the factors that correlate the amount of money with the goods and services, another powerful agent can operate in the marketplace, and modern society deems it necessary to counteract this force. This is **monopoly** or the limitation of competition as a result of the concentration of a product or service in the hands of one or several producers who enter into a price-fixing agreement in order to maximize their profits. A monopoly can emerge not only in the production but also in their distribution. Take, for example, chain megastores that become sole distributors in a certain area.

In general, the emergence of a monopoly is a completely natural process having no ill intent. The most successful producers always push the less successful ones out of the market. They expand their production and begin to dictate the market conditions—above all, the prices for their products. Possession of a patent for a unique device or process can also promote a monopolistic position in the market. The classical Marxist writers saw in this phenomenon the signs of the "decay" of capitalism and its impending downfall and replacement by a new socioeconomic order. Well, this conclusion turned out to be a bit premature.

In the United States, monopolies acquired a special dominance, and the government became the first to act forcefully against them. In the 1920s, Rockefeller's Standard Oil became such a powerful monopoly that the government forcibly broke it up into smaller companies. The United States is considered to have the strictest antimonopoly legislation. How much this regime corresponds to reality is difficult to say. But because of the legislation, multimillion-dollar fines from overreaching monopolists annually pour into government coffers.

In general, though, to a monopolistic growth in prices there are objective inhibiting factors. The first of these is the ability of consumers to pay. Secondly, once a product or service has settled at a high price, it becomes advantageous to search for a cheaper replacement. Another factor is the incentive this provides for the start-up of new companies that can take advantage of the monopoly prices to set up a profitable production line, sell the product at lower prices, and as a result, gain their own share of the market. Modern society, however, is impatient and politicians use this to their advantage. To become popular they promise to "take action", to "put an end to", to "do away with tyranny", etc. What this achieves in the long run is, in fact, a major question.

What should we take away from our discussion so far? Four things:

- money is necessary for the unhindered and uninterrupted exchange of goods and services;

- a governing entity issues the money and strengthens its power if it sticks to rational policies. If the policies depart from the existing economic conditions, the currency might be devalued, prices would increase, and government authority might be weakened;

- the value of money depends on its quantity. Precious metals are probably the best currency, but there are too few natural sources of them to accommodate the modern global turnover of goods and services;

- the amount of money necessary for normal market operations depends not only on the quantity of goods and services in the market, but also on the velocity of turnaround of each currency unit and on availability of credit.

Let's give this last point a bit more consideration.

Credit, Interest and Banks

Professors of economics and finance like to relate the following parable to their students:

> Once there was a traveler who arrived in a small town and decided to stay in a local hotel. At the time there was only one room available, and the traveler paid the manager, let's say, a hundred dollars to reserve the room. Then he went for a walk. The manager of the hotel immediately used the money to pay a local cabinetmaker who had repaired some hotel furniture. The cabinetmaker took this money to the hardware store, from which he had earlier obtained boards, nails, and screws, and paid for them as he had promised. The owner of the hardware store remembered that he was indebted to the owner of the hotel for a dinner in honor of his wife's birthday and took him the one hundred dollars. The traveler, who by this time had walked around the town and discovered that there was nothing noteworthy there, decided to travel on. He came back to the hotel, canceled his room reservation, and got his one hundred dollars back.

Well, you can build such chains of events *ad infinitum*. But what can we learn from this? Goods and services to the tune of $300 were acquired and paid for in full. All but for the one hundred dollars that was returned, unspent, to the original owner. Is this some kind of trick? What's the secret here?

Well, of course, one part of the secret is the speed with which money turns over in the system; we spoke about this earlier. More importantly, however, is the fact that the cabinetmaker, the supply store manager, and the owner of the hotel did not demand immediate payment for their goods or services—they'd known each other a long time. Such a delay in payment is called **credit**. No one knew the traveler, of course, so the hotel owner took his money up front.

Here, a completely extraneous element from a different sphere of human relations is making its way into the discussion of economics: the idea of trust. The whole chain in our story is possible only because the cabinetmaker trusts that the hotel owner will pay him for his work, that the owner of the hardware store trusts the cabinetmaker, and that the hotel owner trusts the owner of the hardware store.

We can even define the exact value of this combined trust: in this case, it is $300.

Let us now look at an example in which the money supply in the state is too restricted. Perhaps the state has been a bit too scrupulous in spending money, or, in an admittedly rare case, the money-minting equipment has broken down. Nevertheless, some people still have money. It could be the money exchangers and simply people who have put money aside (for a daughter's dowry, for a son's education, for building a new home or renovating an old one). While the scarce money in the market can buy more, these people prefer to set it aside because they understand that it will eventually purchase a greater and greater quantity of goods and services. But this presents two problems: first, others do not have such ready cash, and this creates an incentive for criminal behavior; and, secondly, no one knows how long the situation will continue. Suddenly the government wakes up, repairs the appropriate machinery, engineers a war with a neighboring country, and, requiring money for the venture, releases so much money that its value to purchase goods and services decreases. Not only can you no longer afford to build a new house, you cannot even repair the old one.

An urgent need to deposit money safely somewhere and to preserve its value was evident. Also, as commodity exchanges or markets developed within and between states, so too did the demand for the safe movement of money. Who could provide this service? Initially, it was those who had weapons, a military organization, freedom of movement, and some semblance of ethical standards. At one time, the knightly religious orders possessed these qualities. During the Crusades, these knightly orders not only provided (for a fee) an armed escort for pilgrims on their way to the holy sites in Palestine, but also patrolled the important and lucrative trading routes that traversed these regions on the way to India and China. We know that a number of European monarchs entrusted their financial resources to and also borrowed money from the Order of the Knights of the Temple, better known as the Templars. They were made famous in the novels of Walter Scott and in the sensational novel *The Da Vinci Code* by Dan Brown. The Order of the Knights of the Temple rivaled the richest of monarchs, and even the Roman pope, in wealth. As with any business enterprise, however, a successful venture invites competition. The money exchangers and merchants—especially in the Italian littoral city-states of Genoa, Venice, and Florence—created their own financial networks and corresponding security arrangements. At some point, the competition took a rather cruel turn as a result of which the expression "Black Friday" entered the lexicon. On October 13, 1307 (a Friday, as it happens), European monarchs, with the blessing of the pope in Rome, succeeded in inflicting a mortal blow on the Order of the Knights of the Temple. The Templars were arrested, tortured, and executed, and above all, their wealth was confiscated. That conveniently wiped out the royal debt to the order.

As a rule, however, a healthy commercial environment cannot sustain such extreme measures and radical changes in the way power is exerted. Stability and predictability are the normal conditions for carrying out serious financial affairs, although historically there have been exceptions to this rule.

In economics, the development of credit in the marketplace began precisely at the moment when a seller agreed to postpone the buyer's payment. He or she had to do this in order to sell the product and to ensure that the clientele returned to his or her shop when there were few buyers. In such circumstances, commercial credit was born. In exchange for deferred payment, when the sum was substantial, the seller received the buyer's written acknowledgment of the debt. In the best case, there were no limitations or conditions to receipt of the money at some well-defined point in time. The unconditional obligation to repay the money on a specific date is called a promissory note. If the seller then needed money before the date specified on the promissory note, he or she could sell or "negotiate" it with someone who had spare cash at the time. The buyer of the note would not pay the full price on the note, but a discounted amount. That is to say that borrowed money or credit would have its own value, and that value would be less than the value of a cash transaction. Let's say, for example, someone has sold something on credit and has a promissory note from the buyer for one hundred dollars to be repaid in a month. But the seller needs the money immediately. He or she can go to a money exchanger or a private lender, who by definition has spare cash, and negotiate the promissory note. The money lender, depending on his assessment of the risk of receiving—or rather, not receiving—the money at the appointed time of payment, would say that he is prepared to buy the obligation for, let's say, ninety-nine dollars. Thus, his price for ready cash for the month is one dollar or 1 percent of the total sum. This works out to be 12 percent per year, "simple" interest. There is also "compound" interest, but to consider that here would complicate the discussion unnecessarily.

The cost of cash or interest rate per annum depends on a number of factors, the most important being the assessment of the risk involved. This is an everyday concept that has a precise economic meaning and even a definable price.

This worked well when the promissory note was backed by a real transaction and real participants with fully identifiable property. It was less successful when "accommodation bills" (that is, promissory notes that have no substantial security) became the payment instrument. Take, for example, a playboy who passes himself off as the scion of a wealthy family whose miserly parent has kept him on a short leash financially. He goes to a loan shark and says that Daddy is not well and soon all of the estate will be under his control. In the meantime, however, he needs some cash. History is replete with examples of such promissory notes that have become the basis for debtors' prisons, suicides, murders, and similar mayhem.

The promissory note became the means by which producers tried to limit the arbitrary issue of money by the ruler and the interest rates charged by the money exchangers and lenders. A promissory note from one buyer could be used to settle any number of accounts (as in our earlier chain). Everyone who received the promissory note as payment for goods or services could endorse it over to a new seller. Every one of the signatories became a guarantor for the repayment of the debt unless noted otherwise at the time of transfer to the next seller. This gave rise to a whole branch of business law—the law of promissory notes that defined the order of payment as stipulated by the promissory note. Nowadays, sales credit is very common, especially in the United States. However, insofar as the final bill must be paid in currency, it turns out that you cannot avoid hard cash.

We all know that the place to find money, or in any case the biggest cache of money, is in the banks; they are the modern successors to the money exchanges and loan sharks. It is immaterial what the banks are sometimes called—savings banks, credit unions, or whatever. The heart of their business has not changed much. But how and from where do they take this money? Well, we give it to them! Any dollar in the bank is a dollar it has somehow received from us. And that's that. When we hand over to the banks our hard-earned cash, what kind of services are we paying for? Very simply, we are paying for them to preserve and increase it. These services are the main functions of the banking business. Banks do have various other services to sell, but these are the main two.

To fulfill their appointed task, banks, like every other business, must take in more than they give out. It is very easy to see this activity taking place in a bank. You take your money to the bank and deposit it in a term account getting, say, 3 percent interest per year. Then you come to the bank and ask for a loan. The bank lends you the money at an interest rate of 7or 8 percent, or even higher. If the bank is conducting its business properly, it will continue to exist and grow because of this difference in rates of interest. Most banks publish their interest rates so you can easily know what you will get for your deposit and how much you will have to pay the bank for credit.

Banks that simply take money and pay nothing to their depositors certainly do exist. Further, the amounts they accept are above a certain, and usually substantial, amount. In these cases, the service they offer their clients is anonymity; clients, who comprise one category of investors, can keep their money in such banks and no one will be the wiser. These banks are not tiny, and they make entire countries quite wealthy when they locate there. Except for Switzerland, the countries themselves are not noted for their size.

When deciding whether or not to give you a loan, at what amount, for how long, and at what rate of interest, the bank first of all considers the probability of repayment or the risk of non-repayment. This is the critical point in the bank's activity since the fate of the bank depends on a correct assessment of risk. The bank will examine in detail the following factors before they will lend you money: what is your normal income, and what are your normal expenses; what property do you have that can serve as a guarantee of repayment; how much money do you usually keep in the bank; and if you get the loan, what are you planning to spend it on? But that's not all. The bank can look at your age, where you live, who your family is, and where you work and in what capacity. If you are a businessperson and are taking a loan to develop your business, the analysis gets even more complicated. Beyond the personal circumstances, the bank can also assess the general economic situation and the outlook for development. As you can see, it's not a simple matter to make a loan that does not turn out to be a loss to the bank. On the other hand, the bank does have to lend, because without that, there is no reason for its existence.

As banks developed, they began to specialize in different transactions. There are commercial banks that specialize in market transactions, savings banks for working folks and a broad spectrum of the population, and investment banks that deposit funds in various enterprises. The biggest banks combine all these functions. But the foundational activity of all of these is the same: attract funds from outside sources and invest them to make profit.

Here we should note another historical pattern. Successful businesspeople who had acquired and had at their disposal substantial funds of money at some moment started to think: should I save this in a bank that belongs to some stranger, or should I set up my own personal bank so I have better control over the risk of losing my capital? It's not difficult to set up your own bank if you have the money. Hire a knowledgeable, capable staff that have sterling reputations, obtain the necessary licenses, hang out an appropriate sign, install as head of the organization a person who has your complete trust, put your money in the safe, and the business takes off. In the former Soviet Union, this kind of thing was widespread when the leadership decided to wade into a market economy, and bank fraud was in full swing. There was the Russian Railways Bank, the Russian Heating Fuel Bank, the Russian Communications Bank, the Russian Heavy Industries Bank, and so on. Their names clearly indicated who owned these banks and from where they got their money. In the West, this stage in the banking evolution is long past; there, a serious investigation is required in order to establish what bank belongs to whom and where the seed money came from.

In order to conduct a business of the broadest possible scope and largest possible income, banks establish interbank relationships, at first within one state but then moving to an international level. The more numerous the connections with other banks, the better the first bank can serve the needs of its clients. These ties involve both money and reputation. How do these ties get established? Let's say a client of the bank asks that a certain sum of money be paid to his supplier in another city where his bank doesn't have a branch of its own. His bank reaches out to other banks in the destination city and asks that they render this payment service for which they will be paid a certain commission. In return, the bank opens an account in the name of the paying bank and deposits the amount of the payment. Banks that open such accounts for other banks are called "correspondent" banks. As long as there is a risk of losing cash in transport, banks will very happily open such accounts. It goes without saying that one bank will assess the business reputation of the other bank for which the account is opened. The correspondent banks establish limits on unpaid differences in the corresponding accounts and the mutual settlements, and when these limits are exceeded, they settle the account with cash transfers.

Essentially, and with very few exceptions, most of the global cash is in banks. Clearly, in spite of the fact that this situation makes our lives much easier, it also creates serious risks. First, of course, your bank, together with all your money, can evaporate into thin air. This has happened before and happens today. Modern states use a panoply of measures to avoid this situation. There are banking regulations; there are banking licenses to be obtained and there is a central bank that issues them and enforces the rules. In many countries, the public bank deposits are insured. If the bank is a private one, however, the general rules do not apply and the risks stay with the depositors.

There is a serious risk when a bank is not capable of financially sustaining its vital activities. Apart from outright fraud, bankers can adopt mistaken policies or incorrectly assess the lending risks and prevailing economic climate. This is what happened in 2008-2009, and it shook the global financial system to its very core.

It all started when real estate prices began to grow rapidly in the United States. American banks decided that they would profit from lending money to everyone who wanted to buy a house and fulfill the dream of every American family to own their own home. Since ownership of a house itself guaranteed the repayment of the loan (the mortgage), the banks did not much care how the borrowers would find the income to repay it with interest. If the loan payments were not made, the house would be sold at an increased market price, and the bank would not come away the loser. This pursuit of higher and higher returns led to easily available mortgages and ever-increasing prices for real estate since the demand to purchase it on borrowed money was growing. But US banks went a step further.

Around the world, there are disposable funds that banks try to place in the most profitable operations. This search is interminable, and there is an ongoing flow of funds from less profitable to more profitable industries. This creates opportunities for various sorts of market manipulation. Most recently such manipulations with credit and interest rates had serious repercussions for a whole range of countries. American banks sold their loans, which had real estate as collateral. Those who bought up these debt obligations (other banks, pension funds, and other mutual funds) hoped that they were backed by solid collateral, but such was not the case. The market for real estate became saturated rather quickly and prices tumbled. It soon became apparent that many new owners were in no financial position to repay their mortgages. On a massive scale, the recent happy owners of new houses began to part ways with the "American dream". They either declared bankruptcy and stopped paying their debts or simply abandoned the houses and once again took up residence in rental units. Those who bought their debt obligations, being unable to sell the houses for which they had to pay real estate taxes and other carrying costs, incurred huge losses. This tragic situation developed across the entire United States and had global consequences commensurate with the leading role of the American economy in the world.

The crash was not limited to the real estate market; it affected the automobile and other industries as well. The majority of durable goods, including cars, is sold on payment plans. But to buy a car on credit, you must have a good credit history. When you stop paying for your house, the relevant information goes to the credit bureau, which immediately identifies you as a high credit risk and unlikely to repay your debts. After that, not one dealer will negotiate a vehicle sale with you, except for cash or at such a usurious interest rate that you will refuse to make the deal. As a result, car sales declined, and this hit the American companies—Ford, General Motors, and Chrysler—especially hard. They had already ceded their position in the American market to the Japanese and Korean automakers. Fortunately, the American government abandoned all its lofty free enterprise principles and hurriedly rescued its overreaching bankers and unprofitable automobile companies at the expense of all taxpayers.

Another form of credit—credit cards—is widely used in the United States. You can buy almost anything if you have a piece of plastic in your pocket. Usually, for 30 days you do not have to pay for your purchase and you will not have to pay interest. What's the catch? Well, first, usually it is your bank that issues you a credit card, and banks are well aware of how much they can trust you. Secondly, credit cards return a fixed income to the bank that issues them. The seller that takes a credit card as payment pays the bank a fixed percent of the sale (up to 5 percent). But if you are late with your credit card payments, the bank, as punishment, will apply an interest rate that is nothing but highway robbery; you have lost the bank's trust, and the increased risk means that you will pay more to borrow money.

There are also definite advantages for sellers of the goods and services. Payment by credit card instantly puts the money into their accounts. They do not have to bother with cash—counting and recounting it, determining if it is counterfeit, and running to the bank with deposits or hiring security companies to do it. All of this costs money. So it would seem that everyone wins and the marketplace operates smoothly. For a while.

There comes a time when the loss of trust becomes widespread. This is usually tied to the business cycle but on the surface has a very different character: a banking crisis, a panic in the stock market, a crisis in home sales. These phenomena can overlap and reinforce each other so that for millions of people the effect will become truly catastrophic.

At such moments the crisis of trust envelops everyone. Banks do not trust their borrowers. The depositors lose faith in the banks and take out their deposits. Because the banks had invested their clients' funds and are not in a position to fulfill the cash demands at a moment's notice, they simply close their doors, thereby further contributing to the increasing panic. Most goods and services that were purchased on credit cannot be paid for, and the producers incur losses, declare bankruptcy, and dismiss their employees. Having lost their income, the former employees can no longer pay their bills. Bankruptcies proceed on a massive scale and production falls. Prices for essential items take off. History provides us with a number of examples of such economic earthquakes, the most famous being the global crisis of 1929–1934.

So the credit that conveys obvious advantages and convenience to all who participate in the marketplace also bears enormous risks. Fortunately, modern society has learned how to combat such catastrophes or, in any event, to significantly mitigate the consequences.

Now is perhaps the time to talk about the simplest swindle involving money and interest.

You tell one of your acquaintances that you have found an entrepreneur who is using a new technology (or is producing a new product, opening a new oilfield, etc.). This entrepreneur urgently needs money to develop this business, and is ready to pay an annual interest rate of 24 percent on the amount received. You say that you have already invested your savings in that business ($10,000), and every month you get back 2 percent ($200), and this is really not too bad given today's high costs. Your acquaintance is a careful person but says that perhaps he is ready to take a risk. He has $1,000, which he gives you on your word of honor and under threat of serious repercussions if this is some kind of scam. You might tell the tale to five friends and find that you have, say, $5,000 at your disposal. At the end of the month, you carefully pay each depositor his or her 2 percent or twenty dollars. It adds up to only one hundred dollars, and you are left with $4,900. You may be sure that over the next month every one of your friends will talk about this very lucrative investment to at least another five people. Well, generally we are well-intentioned folks, so why not share with our friends such a simple way of making money? Five times five equals twenty-five. Multiply the twenty-five by a thousand if they all are just as careful as your acquaintance and we get $25,000. From this amount we will pay out $520 (20 x 26) at the end of the month. Perhaps now is the time to open an office and hire a secretary and a bookkeeper; at this rate after three months you will have on hand no less than $100,000. The main thing is that you pay the accrued interest on time and, should someone need their money back, give it to them without hesitation. But such cases will be few indeed—remember, there is a 24 percent interest rate.

So now you have built a financial "pyramid" or a "Ponzi" scheme. You can give it a pleasant-sounding name—for example, MMM. (Oh wait, that one is already taken. Pick something else.) After another couple of months you could advertise in the newspapers or on the radio and TV, rent more impressive offices, set up a vault for the never-ending flow of cash, hire a security company, expand the workforce, and continue to ramp up the scale of the operation.

The day will surely come when your investors will wake up and realize that something is not right. They will start to wonder when it would be best to ask for the return of their money. But the 2 percent return on investment every month goes a long way to stifling their common sense. It has often been demonstrated that greed trumps common sense. You are simply playing with the completely understandable desire of every one of us to get something for nothing.

The last thing you have to decide is when is the right moment to close forever the doors of your money-collection operation. You should have, with some foresight, taken out citizenship in some exotic country to which you would transfer your funds (preferably a country with a mild climate and no extradition treaties with foreign jurisdictions—such countries still do exist).

An interesting question is: Where are the natural limits of growth in such a scheme? With a legally established business supported by a sterling reputation and cordial international relations, you can take money not only from individual citizens but also from legitimate businesses, including banks, trust funds, and even the government.

To give your business a more respectable look, you could lower your rate of return to 12 percent, and, all things being equal, this will not turn off those who want to entrust you with their own or someone else's money. But there comes a time when all the cash available on the global market is in your hands. This would be the beginning of the end. When the last schoolchild on earth has skipped school breakfast and the old peasant woman has taken the pittance set aside for her funeral and they have sent their small nest eggs to you for safekeeping, then you can put an end to it. Inasmuch as you are paying the highest rate of return, there is nowhere for you to deposit the money under your control so that you can receive a higher rate of return. And there are no more new investors. Your capital begins to dwindle with greater or lesser speed, depending on your tastes. Given the global nature of your operations, there are unlikely to be any places left where you can retire in peace. Well, maybe there are some, but you do not want to settle there.

Stocks, Bonds and the Stock Exchange

Let's take a look at tranquil economic times when everything is going along in an orderly fashion. Producers are offering their goods and services; buyers are happily purchasing them on credit and paying off their accounts. No one in his or her economic niche is taking special risks or posing a threat for the established chain of trust and exchange.

Then along comes an especially successful entrepreneur who wants to grow his or her business. The producer's goods or services are in very high demand, and buyers or clients who show up at the end of the day are more and more likely to leave empty-handed. But for every buyer who leaves without a purchase, there is a corresponding loss of income. What's worse, the buyer might go to the competition. Who would want that? One thing is clear: the successful business must grow. Additional facilities must be rented or built; new workers must be hired. But all of this costs money. Earlier we saw that it is possible, of course, to borrow money from a bank or another lender. But any of these lenders want their cut as a percent of the credit extended and to wash their hands of any further involvement. On the other hand, our entrepreneur still doesn't know how the business will expand and how to repay the debt with interest. What can be done to share the upcoming risks and thus reduce them?

Entrepreneurs are different from other people in that they find a way to turn a profit rather quickly. And to do so, they take advantage of the weaknesses of ordinary folk who generally like to make some extra cash without expending too much effort or risking too much. One fine day we learn that a well-known, successful entrepreneur wants to expand the business and is looking for investors. The future profits will be split in proportion to their contribution. This news, combined with the rather low rate of return we are getting from our deposit at the bank, raises our interest. Now suppose that from our own trips to the store, we know that this producer turns out quality products that are in demand. Why would we not participate? What would be the real risk? Would this entrepreneur work to his or her own detriment? The entrepreneur then releases to the market one thousand promises to share in future profits. Last year the company's profit was, let's say, $100,000; if the business continues to function in the same way, every **share** will get one hundred dollars of the profit. The shares are now selling for $1,000 each, so the expected rate of return is 10 percent. Not bad! Right now, the bank is paying us only 3 percent for our term deposit of $100,000. Why, for that money we could buy one hundred shares. What would be better:$3,000 or $10,000? OK, just a minute, maybe it won't be 10 percent like last year; maybe 6 percent. Make haste! The logic of this is quite simple and persuasive.

The definition of a share (or stock) bears repeating: a share is nothing more than a promise to share in any future profit. That's why when an enterprise goes bankrupt and liquidates the business, you can count on only an ownership share of the remaining assets. But in such circumstances, the remaining assets are so tiny that it's not worth seriously thinking about them. The people who buy shares rarely think about what happens if the company in which they invest money goes bankrupt.

From the point of view of the entrepreneur issuing the shares, this is a very productive thing to do. You are immediately getting money from share sales but are obliged to share only the future profit. The payout from the shares is called **dividends.** A whole range of specific technicalities accompany the issuance and sale of shares. You don't have to offer the shares to the general public on the **stock exchange**; they can be offered only to members of the family, to acquaintances, or to other entrepreneurs and bankers. Under these conditions, you are not required to publish your annual financial accounts after they have been verified by independent auditors.

Issuing shares on the stock exchange can be done only through stockbrokers, and shares can be of various types, the most common of which are: privileged (that is, those that guarantee a certain dividend or give additional rights to their owners) and common shares (shares that give no guarantees or special rights). All shareholders may participate in the affairs of the company by attending shareholder meetings and voting, where the number of votes is equal to the number of shares held. This, however, does not change the essence of what we are discussing: you, as a shareholder, have the right to receive dividends and participate in the general shareholder meetings. Nothing more than that. Thus, participation by all of the shareholders in the running of the business may be limited, and major decisions, including the fate of the company, are left in the hands of the actual owners. The question of who are the real owners is such a broad subject that it demands its own branch of research.

The issue, purchase, and sale of stocks proved to be so attractive for the business community that the activities became broadly prevalent. At the end of the 1970s, during my first trip to the United States, I noted that the driver of the company car that took our team from worksite to worksite assiduously read the morning paper (it goes without saying that he did this when the car was stuck in traffic) and was quite emotional about it, although the paper itself was strictly business (*The Wall Street Journal*, I guess). I was, of course, surprised by such interest and, seizing an opportune moment, asked him what was going on. "Well, something is wrong with my stocks" was his unexpected reply. "They are all over the map, and I have to figure out why. "

Such wide participation by the general populace in the financial affairs of industry gives rise to a lot of myths, the upshot of which is that, even without a socialist revolution, the nature of private ownership has changed and transformed itself into a different social phenomenon. Let's not be distracted here by questions of abstract theory but rather attend to more practical questions.

Widespread buying and selling of stocks on the market has led to the emergence of a special type of occupation: market speculation. How does this work? In any serious contemporary newspaper, there is a section with long columns of abbreviations and numbers. These represent companies and the price (quotations) for their stocks. The prices usually are for the first and last purchases of the day. All transactions go through stockbrokers who make a commission on the sale. Let's say, for example, the stock price for "ABC" company was one hundred dollars, and for some reason (the advice of a specialist, personal study of the company's business, simple intuition or whim), you are certain that sooner or later it will be higher. You buy some ABC shares and, if your forecast is correct, keep them until you can sell them for profit. Such a purchase is a bet on a rising market, and having successfully completed the transaction, you have become a "bull", the New York stock market jargon for buyers who bet on a rising stock market.

You can also bet on a falling market, and it works like this: Suppose you need cash or have a feeling that the price of the stocks you have will go down. To unload them you start offering the shares for the price lower than the latest quotes. You have become a "bear", that is, someone who bets on a falling market.

There are more complex transactions on stock exchanges, but let's not complicate the discussion.

The sales and purchases of stocks are usually numbered in thousands, and the profits and losses are commensurate.

A word about losses in these operations. Only brokers don't incur them. A broker's commission is independent of the outcome of the transactions, so brokers do not realize a loss. Not bad. If you are thinking about becoming a broker, well, go ahead. But you need to know that to participate in stock exchanges costs millions of dollars and demands sterling recommendations from current participants. So this is serious business, as is everything that is connected with large amounts of money in the modern world.

Today there are a number of stock markets with a multibillion-dollar turnaround. There are two in New York, and one each in London, Paris, Tokyo, and Milan. Markets in other countries are a bit smaller. There are also commodities exchanges where bulk goods—oil, rubber, grain, base metals—are quoted, and there are currency exchanges where different world currencies are traded. With the emergence of the Internet, it has become possible to complete a trade while just sitting at the computer. All these markets rest on one principle: the opportunity to make (and lose) money.

Clearly, stock trading offers a broad scope for all sorts of fraud. Historically there are many examples of fortunes made and lost in a blink of an eye. Most frequently, a chance to hit the jackpot crops up when you have information that, while not available to other traders, can influence the price of shares. Any number of events can affect share price that at first blush have no direct connection, such as an earthquake in Japan or a flu epidemic in Europe. And there are firms that specialize in understanding the effects of various events and in selling their analyses and forecasts. As the ubiquitous journalists have it, information is the mother of intuition. Especially valuable is any information connected with the leadership of companies listed on the stock exchange. Who is meeting with whom over business lunches? What is the latest cocktail party gossip? Why is so-and-so ill and how seriously? And you would stand to make a pretty penny if someone shared with you information about the release of a profitable new product line or a future corporate merger.

An entire legal code of conduct has been developed to govern the business affairs of the owners and employees of companies listed on the stock exchange and to regulate the transactions of the traders and stockbrokers. This has been created so that the many people who invest their savings in, and hope to get rich from, the stock markets are not frightened off by the possibility of being swindled. Dedicated oversight bodies ensure adherence to the regulations governing the markets, and their violation is a criminal offense. Regardless of the rigor of enforcement, however, from time to time we learn of cases of "insider trading", where proprietary information has been used to get rich on the stock market. Well-known personalities, if caught, may pay huge fines and even go to jail. It is thought that there are many more such cases than have come to light—the temptation is too great and the likelihood of getting caught, too small.

On the other hand, there are plenty of legal ways to manipulate stock market prices and to do so requires a substantial amount of money. Let's take, for example, a company whose "capitalization" (the ratio of the cost of shares to the value of its assets) is completely equitable or even a little undervalued. Following your orders, your stockbroker begins to buy up its shares for you. The market is very responsive to all changes in circumstance, and the stock price begins to rise. Other "players" conclude that the initial buyer has information about a possible growth in company revenues and hence in the dividends to the shareholders. The shares reach the price at which you anticipate the highest return, and at this moment you order your stockbroker to sell them off. As a rule, the largest players in the market give their brokers a standing order: buy shares in such-and-such a company if the price falls below a specified level and sell them if it rises above a specified level. To do this successfully, it is important to understand the market and how to work out appropriate tactics of buying and selling. Mastering these techniques is not the easiest thing to do and takes years of experience in the market and a good bit of money lost through bad decisions.

Stock market indices and their movements are featured prominently in the business sections of the mass media. Every stock exchange has its own index, or even several indices—NYSE, NASDAQ, FTSE, NIKKEI, and so forth. The indices show the volume of sales and the general price trends Monday through Friday. The general trend is like the average body temperature for hospital patients. Someone has a high fever and someone else is already in the morgue, so the average temperature is "normal". Let's say the DowJones index falls. This does not mean that the value of your particular shares has dropped. The index jumps about on a daily basis, but it is the dynamic of the index over some period of time that reflects the general state of the economy. Well, what does "the general state of the economy" mean? More on this in the next chapter. At this point let's not get distracted by dubious speculation; instead let's take a look at bonds and how they function in the business world.

Bonds are also debt obligations, but they last for a set period and pay a fixed interest. The person who buys bonds does not expect a share of either the income or the assets of the enterprise that issues them. He or she knows only that the interest will be paid regularly and that in due time the bond will return its face value. This would seem to be a reliable business deal, especially since bonds are issued not only by companies but also by public authorities—federal, state, and municipal governments. Well, as they say, "the devil is in the details". And with bonds, there are a number of significant details: Who is issuing them? For what time period? At what rate of interest? For what price? Let's start with this last question, price.

Suppose "XZY" company issues its bonds at an annual rate of 6 percent interest and with a maturity date of one year. Each bond has a face value—for the sake of argument, $1,000. After one year, you will receive $1,060 for each bond purchased. At what price can the company expect to sell its bonds? Suppose that banks are currently offering 5 percent per year on one-year term deposits. That is to say, having deposited $1,000 in the bank for one year, you will receive $1,050 at the end of the year. The sensible thing would be to buy the bonds because to get $60 from the bank deposit at 5 percent annually, you would have to invest not $1,000 but $1,200. The bond seller understands this and therefore sells the bonds for $1,005, which means you do not have a return of sixty dollars, but only fifty-five dollars ($1,060 minus $1,005). Even so, purchasing the bond makes sense: for every thousand dollars, you receive five dollars more than you would from the bank.

During this time, another factor is affecting bond prices: the price of shares. Suppose that the annual average return (dividend plus whatever price increase) for all shares on the stock exchange is expected to be 10 percent and the average price of a share is one hundred dollars. Thus the annual return on $1,000 worth of shares is one hundred dollars. So, investing your $1,000 in the 6 percent bond, which returns only $1,060, makes no sense. But if you were to pay only $950 for the bond and thus receive $110 in income ($60 + $50), well, that is a whole different ball game. So you can see that the movement of stock prices affects the price of bonds. The lower the share index, the higher the price of bonds. But the upper limit of the price of bonds, as we have discovered, is determined by the bank rate for deposits.

We have already mentioned the maturity date of bonds, and this also affects their appeal in the marketplace. The shorter the maturity date, the better; there are fewer factors that can decisively change and influence the price (i.e., the stock price and the bank rates). Even more important, however, is the entity issuing the bonds. It's one thing if it's a government body; it's entirely another if it is some hitherto unknown company. While it is true that a bond can be redeemed unconditionally if the company should declare bankruptcy, redemption can be a long, drawn-out process. So a credit rating for the entity issuing the bonds determines how attractive they are in the market. Specialized independent agencies determine the credit rating; the best known of these are Moody's, Standard & Poor, and Fitch. How independent these agencies are and from whom are questions that have yet to be answered, but the fact remains that they can decrease the credit rating of even government bonds. Not long ago such a fate befell US bonds.

Standard & Poor lowered the credit rating of the government's debt from AAA (the highest possible rating). There was an immediate corresponding drop in the prices of American bonds, which displeased the government no end. The authorities were even preparing to sue over calling into question the reputation of the pillar of the global economy. Then the furor somehow just faded away.

Imagine what kind of nervous tension torments people who have significant financial resources at their disposal. Where are these funds safe from inflation, racketeering, bank failure and any other misfortune? You can, of course, hire personal advisors, but even they get things wrong sometimes. We should feel really sorry for people with a lot of money.

And then, on top of it all, there are the economic crises! What are these about?

Economic Crises

There are all sorts of economic crises: overproduction, financial, real estate, and on and on. They can be local or global. The most serious crises are comprehensive in nature. That is, each exacerbates the others; they affect all sectors of the economy and impact the entire global economic system.

It is generally accepted that crises are associated with a capitalist economy, but it is probably more correct to say that they are connected with market production—with goods produced for trade. The source of the crises is such a lack of demand for your goods or services that the price at which you can sell your product is insufficient to cover your expenses. There are various reasons for this that may relate to your own industry or to general consumer interest.

When producers and consumers are linked by lines of credit, a crisis will become one of confidence.

Economists have agreed to define a growing economy as one in which demand for goods and services is growing at a consistent pace and production is concomitantly expanding. When demand exists but is not growing and, as a result, neither is production, the economy is at a standstill. This is a state of stagnation. Worse, when demand is falling and marketing goods and services has become difficult, recession sets in. An extreme state of recession is called a crisis. Political economists long ago established that the economies develop cyclically, which we can show graphically:

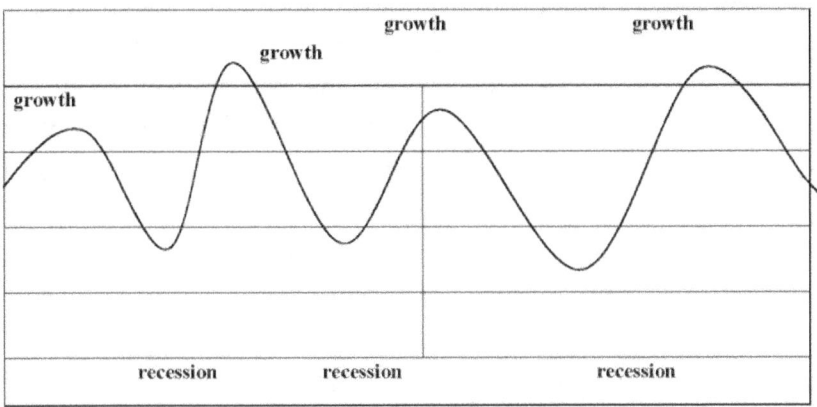

General economic recession certainly does not mean that some sectors cannot be expanding. And in some industries, cyclicality is significantly muted by their nature—for example, hairdressing or, unfortunately, burial services.

Let's examine more closely some characteristics of the two trends of an economic cycle.

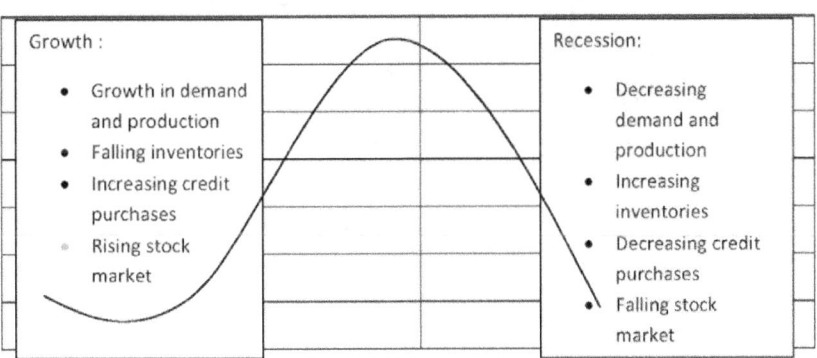

Growth :
- Growth in demand and production
- Falling inventories
- Increasing credit purchases
- Rising stock market

Recession:
- Decreasing demand and production
- Increasing inventories
- Decreasing credit purchases
- Falling stock market

During a period of stagnation, of course, it does not make sense to issue new stock in order to expand production. Businesses will issue new stock at this time only to top up cash reserves in order to survive hard times. At the same time, the quantity of money available for market speculation decreases as does the appetite for risks. The supply of stocks already on the market grows since everyone now wants to have ready cash. Likewise, the chances are that company's income and dividends paid on stock are also falling. In this situation, one can reasonably expect the general decline of the stock market. "Well, so what?" you ask. "Producers, by issuing and selling stock, have already gotten their money for expansion. Market speculators, depending on whether they are bulls or bears, have made or lost their money. Those are the risks they took. What's the problem for the rest of us?"

The problem is that the crisis can become deeper and more personal in a number of rather dangerous ways. For example, an industrialist, having decided to expand the business, cannot do so because no one is buying its stock. Pension funds and other organizations, having deposited their financial resources in stocks that pay no dividend and are sold at great discount, are unable to pay retirees' pensions and dividends; the retirees' purchasing power falls. Banks that have bought the shares now have less value from them on their balance sheets and must decrease the interest they pay on deposits while increasing the interest on extended credit. Once again, both producers and depositors are affected. Overall distrust in the system grows and with it, a reduction in demand for goods and services, which intensifies the crisis even further.

In general, an all-out pursuit of ready cash typifies a period of crisis. Accounts must be paid so that trust is not lost and credit worthiness is maintained. But the revenue stream is subject to increased risk. One of your customers, to whom you have sold goods on credit, goes bankrupt. Someone else loses his or her job. The chains of sales volume and credit become sufficiently brittle so that the weakest link snaps and causes serious failure throughout the system. For this reason, crises are usually accompanied by a "run" on the banks—depositors, forgetting that there are advantages to keeping their money where it can earn interest, begin to withdraw their deposits. Any given bank, however, has already reallocated the funds, lending them out at a higher interest rate and leaving in reserve only enough to cover their depositors' daily withdrawals. A run on the bank is every banker's worst nightmare. There are only two ways to stop it: ensure that depositors can withdraw their funds or close the doors of the bank, which is equivalent to killing the bank.

How does a crisis get started? What kind of shock will initiate a transition from peak business activity to a recession? One contemporary Russian researcher has made a connection between crises and solar activity. Carrying this a bit further, another Russian researcher has theorized that there is a connection between solar activity and global upheavals such as world wars and major revolutions. We won't quibble with these profound deductions. The contours of every concrete event are different. The baker, having taken loans from bankers and builders to expand his or her bakery and increase the output of more expensive rolls and fancy buns to meet the growing demand, suddenly finds the store's shelves full at the end of the day. Revenue falls off, and one of the links in the chain of product turnover and creditworthiness begins to snap. Add a number of these situations together and you get the beginning of a crisis. In every case, an economic crisis starts with overproduction and the inability of current purchasing power to absorb all the goods and services on the market. If you expand credit to increase the purchasing power of your clients, you will simply prolong and deepen the consequences of the crisis.

If economists have established the cyclicality and frequency of economic crises, why not get on top of the situation and take precautionary measures? This is a very reasonable question. Let's say that you sell stocks just before their price falls, or you withdraw money from the bank before there is a general run. This is what the professional market players try to do. They watch the multitude of economic indicators and shift their money from stock to bonds, from bonds to real estate, from real estate to stocks, from one currency to another, from gold to stocks, from cash to gold, from country to country, and so on. They hire whole teams of well-paid specialists in order to make the most advantageous decisions. But even so, they suffer losses. They cannot predict what other market players of their scale will do. They cannot know where to find the weak link that will break the chain of goods-money-credit, a break that will bring the consequences of a general loss of the trust on which a dynamic market depends. For these market players, the crisis may mean losing only part of their substantial assets, but for the rest of us, this can be a considerable blow. We might take comfort in knowing that the markets, and therefore the players, cannot exist without the production and consumption of goods and services. And we are the consumers. Were we all to go bankrupt, lose our jobs, and limit consumption of goods and services to a bare minimum, accumulated capital would lose its ability to create profit and will be subject to a real risk of loss in the ensuing social upheaval.

Yet another question arises: If economic crisis is the result of human activity, why can't we take steps to redirect or correct this activity in order to avoid a crisis? It is, after all, not a natural disaster but the result of individual and group human actions. As it turns out, this is possible. Historically we know that there are quite successful ways of combating crises. In the countries where the state owned the means of production, economic crises did not exist. All production was centrally planned and allocated. These states targeted general levels of consumption and, based on their political goals, centrally designated production and inventory levels. In conditions where consumption is strictly controlled and limited, however, there is little incentive to increase work productivity. When this is combined with ambitious geopolitical strategies and other noneconomic factors, the breakup of the system is inevitable as we've seen in the case of the Soviet economy. Could it have been otherwise? Hard to say. But elements of state ownership and central planning have worked and even now continue to work successfully in a number of countries that do not call themselves socialist. These countries simply do not establish geopolitical goals that require excessive resources at the expense of personal consumption of their citizens.

But what if in a time of crisis we inject additional money into the economy? Everybody is looking for cash at that time. Nobody has enough of it. Let's print more dollars or euros and give them to consumers as salaries, bonuses, or just donations. The consumers will bring them to the stores to buy goods and services, demand will rise, and production can be expanded. That is the end of the crisis! Nice and simple! But on this road significant dangers confront us. First, demand and production have physical limits. Producers have at their disposal only limited stocks of raw materials and production capacities. Consumers also cannot expand their appetites endlessly. Even if part of the additional money does not enter the market but goes to savings accounts, the banks will have to circulate that money in the form of loans and credit. This way, the injected money will grow faster than the goods and services in the market. This will lead to inflation and price increase. That, in turn, weakens the trust in the government that issues the money whose value is falling. Now we step into the area of politics and have a shaky government whose opponents are only waiting to seize the power. And the hands that grab the power, as history shows, may be of questionable cleanliness. Add to this situation international factors and it can deteriorate into serious conflicts, such as world wars and other catastrophes.

The organic development of a perfectly free market cannot proceed without crises. They are natural regulators in an otherwise chaotic process. The freer the market activity, the more onerous are the consequences of crisis corrections to imbalances in production and demand. You can find evidence of this in archival photographs from the late 1920s and early 1930s. There you will see on the streets of the richest cities of the planet queues of decently dressed people who are awaiting their share of broth from the soup kitchen. There you will see wheat and even coffee beans used for fuel because there was no market for them. Let us sincerely hope that humanity has drawn the right lessons from such extreme situations.

Now let's turn away from the unpleasant aspects of the cyclical development of the economy and spend some time on yet another significant player in the economic process: the state.

State Budget and State Debt: Economics and Politics

What distinguishes governments from other players in economic relationships is the fact that a state establishes the rules that govern everyone else and then ensures that these rules are followed. How poorly or how well they carry this out will affect everyone.

The state needs money to exist. We have already established that although the state can issue money (print it or mint it), there is a real limit to what it can do. This limit is the sum total of available goods and services. To issue money too much beyond this limit is to invite trouble for the state. To avoid this, the government must keep a strict account of money issued and ensure that its value is maintained.

Having come to power (regardless of whether it was a result of democratic election or government coup), the leaders must immediately calculate the amount of money they need so that their power is not weakened. Accountants, hired by the state to work in the treasury or the finance ministry, have the job of calculating how much money is necessary for upkeep of the military, police, courts, prisons, and other government institutions. Once this task is completed, the accountants must determine how to raise the necessary funds. Planned expenditures and income (usually annual) make up the state **budget**. The primary difference between a state budget and that of any family—besides its size, of course—is that the average family looks first to income and, from this, plans its expenditures. The state does it the other way around, first calculating how much money it needs and then from where it should take the funds.

It turns out that there are not many options: print money, confiscate it from whoever has it, sell something, or take it as a loan from whoever is willing to lend. The first course of action is the easiest but, as we have already seen, it runs up against the real problem of inflation. The second choice, the most unpopular with the general population, is taxes. The third option is to provide additional services to the public at a charge. The fourth, issuing government bonds, requires that the state pay interest and repay the debt. If that were not to happen, any bonds subsequently issued would find no buyers.

Generally, the government uses all of these techniques, and depending on the choice of the moment, we can determine what economic policy the state is pursuing. Yet with any policy, the government cannot avoid engaging in certain sectors of the economy. Take, for example, the country's highway system; the development of this network benefits the general economy. Would a private company—or even a group of companies—take up the work? No way! Because the *raison d'être* of any enterprise is profit. There is no way to know when and how much profit one can gain from investing in building highways. None of this work would get done without state involvement. Let's take another example: communication systems. From their very beginning, postal and telegraph services were one of the most important state functions. Don't forget that both the transportation and communications networks have military value and, from the state's point of view, entrusting them to private hands would be risky.

What are the factors that determine the economic policy of a government? There are many. Among them are national culture, history, natural resources, climatic conditions, education, population size and density, and the level of social development. In today's world, all factors interact in complicated ways and at times perplex even the most analytical of minds. Consider the recent example of the bizarre state of the former Libyan Arabic Socialist Jamahiriya—well, we knew it simply as Libya. For all intents and purposes, Libya had almost built a communist society based on its oil revenues. Most of the needs of the population were met from the state budget since, with the exception of the demands of the family of the leader, the general populace did not require anything very extravagant. But this turned out to be insufficient to guarantee the primary function of state power: namely, its ongoing survival. We could, of course, argue about the role of outside interference in Libyan ways, but it seems that something was fundamentally wrong with its economic policy too.

The art of the government-in-power's politics consists of the ability to balance competing interests and smooth over the imbalances that threaten the society. Also, government's policy can facilitate the growth of production of goods and services or inhibit this growth. How? The most widespread method is through the level of taxation. If taxes are low, the government has less money to spend on activities that don't immediately create additional goods and services or are just extravagant. The population keeps more money to spend on goods and services. Increases in demand create the conditions for expansion of industry. Clearly, a majority of the population would only welcome such developments. The growth of specific industries can be stimulated by providing them with tax incentives.

Why, you ask, would one hinder growth? Who benefits from that? There is arguably one danger in this. Recall the crisis we discussed above? Unrestrained growth in production sooner or later will lead to overproduction in one or several sectors, and general contentment will turn into general panic. Collapse then leads to a decline in tax receipts and a deficit in the state budget. To compensate, the government is forced to print more money. Inflation follows and adds to general uncertainty.

In states considered prosperous but not luxurious—foremost among them, the Scandinavian countries—the governments heavily tax income. In return, they guarantee the people a high quality of life and stability. Perhaps this approach is a peculiarly Scandinavian national trait, but in the midst of economic earthquakes, these countries are calm and peaceful. Moreover, if, like oil-rich Norway, they have surplus natural resources, then in general we can consider them "a paradise on earth". Well, the climate is not exactly paradisiacal, especially in winter, but as the Finns say, "There is no bad weather; there is only poor clothing. " And they know about bad weather.

In a different scenario, let's look at a hypothetical state that seemingly does not want to weigh down its citizens with high taxes. Its citizens are loath to part with their money, especially for services that they think they can provide themselves. Maintenance of law and order is the first service that citizens normally expect from the authorities. In this case, however, the majority of citizens decided not to rely on the state but to purchase firearms with no particular difficulty, in whatever quantity and of whatever quality they desired. Undoubtedly openly carrying such weapons facilitates a more polite interaction in public places and makes robbery a bit more problematic. Arms manufacturers are especially happy about such weaponized peacefulness. The corresponding legal provisions can even be fixed in the foundational law of the country. The problem is that anyone who is under psychological or emotional stress, or has extreme political views, and has a rapid-fire weapon can create the havoc of actual military actions. To make it worse, little kids like to imitate TV shows and games and, unsupervised, are not always careful where they point their parents' unattended weapons.

On the other hand, in Switzerland, the country with high taxes, where weapons possession is almost universal, there are remarkably few unfortunate incidents. But this is part of their weapon handling culture dating back to the time of national hero William Tell, who was able to shoot an apple from his son's head with a crossbow when forced to do so by the overreaching local authorities.

But let us get back to the issues of state and money.

With the development of human society and a complex economic system, it became apparent that the state would have to introduce some kind of supervision over the printing of money to prevent increasing instability across the state institutions. As we saw previously, it is necessary to pay attention to the appearance and development of inflationary indicators. To entrust this oversight to the government is not a very safe thing to do; the government will always find urgent reasons to mint a little more money. In countries with the most advanced economic and social systems, business communities have found that the amount of money in circulation and the amount of credit should be controlled by a central bank whose activities would be independent of the decisions of the government. In the United States, the Federal Reserve is such an institution.

So what does the central bank do to regulate money in circulation? First, it establishes bank regulations that limit member banks' risks.

These regulations can also affect the amount of credit made available to consumers—another factor that can cause inflation. Secondly, a member bank can turn to the central bank when there is pressure on its cash holdings. Necessary short-term funds can be provided at an established, and usually very low, rate of interest. The central bank establishes the interest rate at which it lends money based on its assessment of the economic situation and the level of inflation. If the economy is expanding and the production of goods and services is increasing, the bank may raise the interest rate to make credit more expensive, thus limiting the possibility of overproduction and decreasing the possibility of a crisis. If the economy is stagnant, the interest rate is lowered, banks are encouraged to expand lending, and entrepreneurs get credit at a lower rate.

To what extent is the central bank independent of the government? This is an important question. The head of the central bank is usually nominated by the chief executive (prime minister, president, etc.) and confirmed by the legislative body. This legislative body (Parliament, Congress, etc.), among other things, is designed to control the power of the administration to increase spending. This control, however, is weakened by the very nature of political power. Take any candidate for political office—a parliament, for example. The candidate, needing to attract more voters than the competitor, promises voters more opportunities to earn money or receive state benefits (pensions, medical insurance, etc.) depending on the prevailing interests of his or her constituency.

Most of these promises are never kept after an election. Well, many promises will get you universal love but along comes the time for reelection, and when that love is faltering because of unfulfilled promises, something must be done. It's just the time to push through government financing for local projects: a bridge, a road, a military base, or a government building. All of these projects become the subject of cutthroat haggling when state budgets are being discussed, but the result is that expenditures of the state budget grow. Since this growth must be covered by receipts, taxes increase (an undesirable measure if you want to be popular), money is borrowed, or state bonds are issued, and everyone waits to see how much demand there is for them. If the interest rate on the bonds is attractive compared to other forms of investment for available cash—bank deposits, stocks, real estate, gold, or antiques—they will be in demand. But a high interest rate for bonds means that the state once again must increase its expenditures for interest payments. The result is growing state debt.

Where is the limit to growth in state debt? As with an individual or a company, it is defined by the trust that a creditor has in someone's ability to repay a debt. If the government runs up too much debt in comparison with its receipts, no one will want to extend it credit. When this happens, what follows? The state will have to print more money, which devalues, since there is no increase in goods and services in the market place. Lending money becomes less profitable, or the interest rate takes off in order to offset the losses from inflation. In extreme cases, the government will have to halt repayment of its debt altogether. This is called **default** or state bankruptcy, and it is the pensioners and state employees who are likely to suffer. State-owned industries and property may be sold. Anyone who has lent the government money will also suffer. All of this has a negative impact on consumers' demand and on the state of the economy as a whole. Generally, a government that has become bankrupt would resign, but this does not make life easier for its creditors.

Besides the internal difficulties, the government faces external ones. Every government must manage two sets of relationships: relationships with its citizens and relationships with other states. Now let's examine how these two sets of relationships interact in the economic sphere.

But first, recall that in a market economy where business processes develop organically, the role of the government is limited. It can ameliorate economic slumps but cannot quash them entirely. Anyone who blames the prime minister and the government or the president for the poor state of the economy (high unemployment, low rates of industrial growth or recession) without rejecting the principles of the free market is dissembling in order to achieve popularity or realize his or her own political goals. Further limiting the role of the government is the fact that the economy of any one country is connected with the economies of a multitude of other countries whose governments are also trying to influence the economic processes to whatever extent possible.

Foreign Trade and the Balance of Trade

Trade between various countries started at the very moment when the first states appeared. Before that, of course, the various tribes traded among themselves. When, because of nature, climate, culture, etc., one tribe produced more of certain goods than it needed, it was advantageous to trade them with other tribes for other goods that it lacked. The benefit was obvious to everyone.

Gradually, with the development of the division of labor, it became apparent that there were members of society who, while not skilled in the production of goods, were nonetheless successful in exchanging them for profit. Also, special places for exchange sprang up, such as fairgrounds and trading cities. They developed especially quickly when located close to waterways, the easiest means of travel and transportation.

Merchants were the people who began to specialize in commerce. They also showed themselves to be good sources of information about lands near and far and the most valuable sources of income for the state treasury. Consider, for example, the medieval rulers whose countries lay on the major trade routes and whose merchants could bring into Europe fine and curious goods from India and China. First, some of these goods found their way into the hands of the rulers and, more specifically, the hands of their wives and favorite daughters. Secondly, customs duties were imposed on the merchandise. In return, the merchants could count on their personal security and on that of their goods in the territory of that state or city. Of course, not all tribute was taken by the rulers; in some places the young gentlemen of the highway took their share, a state of affairs about which the government was quite intolerant. Modern customs agencies are the direct descendants of the old tollgates that local rulers depended on to collect levies and duties.

International trade paid off handsomely and became the stimulus for significant geographic discoveries. We know that Christopher Columbus did not set out to discover America. And yet this is the discovery for which he is famous, because it became imperative to find new routes to the source of the exotic wares of the East. As a result, whole continents were almost stripped of their indigenous inhabitants. The ancient Inca and Aztec civilizations were swept from the face of the earth and their riches used to promote the Industrial Revolution in Europe. Gold taken from the New World was turned into coins and put to profitable use. The same situation occurred in Asia and Africa. And in Russia, the conquest of Siberia, having received the blessing of Tsar Ivan the Terrible, was carried out at the behest of the Stroganovs' trading enterprise.

Given the profitability of overseas and land expeditions, governments began to take the most active interest in them, mostly in the form of military-political patronage. Having come late to the theft of the golden treasure of America, the English queen began to give her sailors license to plunder the Spanish ships that were carrying those riches to Europe. Famous pirate Francis Drake, for his exploits on the high seas, received the noble title of Knight of the Garter. Nor did French royalty lose any time in taking action. But once the English crown had gotten its hands on the resources of the Hindustan peninsula, whose wealth had to be transported home around all of Africa, Great Britain began actively to combat piracy.

Contemporary global trade is quite civilized. It is regulated by international trade laws and various bilateral and multilateral agreements. Underlying international trade is a simple principle: buy goods where they are the cheapest, and sell them where they are the most expensive. Don't forget to take into account the transportation costs—cheap goods get expensive when the transportation is costly.

In principle, there is everything to be gained by trading internationally. Bringing in goods from other countries (**import**) meets the demand that could not be satisfied domestically or that would require goods so expensive that no one could afford to buy them. Sale of one's own goods abroad (**export**) provides an opportunity for expanding production and increasing employment and profit.

There is an interesting fact about transportation costs. According to global trade statistics, when you compare the cost of all exports with the cost of all imports, there is a difference. Imports are roughly 10 percent more expensive than exports. Why the difference? After all, the goods imported by all countries are no more than the goods exported by other countries. The explanation is found in that export figures, are calculated without regard for the cost of insurance and transport. This basis of calculation is called FOB (free on board). On the other hand, import statistics include the cost of goods plus insurance and transport or freight. This is called CIF (cost, insurance, and freight). That's the reason for the difference. Incidentally, customs offices, in addition to collecting customs duties, are a source of import/export statistics, which are an important component of global economic statistics.

Very few countries in the modern world can do well without external trade. If we take the total volume of globally produced goods and services (which was roughly about US$70 trillion in 2008) and the total volume of exports in the same year (about US$16 trillion), we can see that about 23 percent of all production was exported and imported. And this share continues to increase. Even those countries that are self-sufficient in natural resources lack some goods or can purchase them more cheaply than they can be produced domestically.

For some countries, economic development is not possible without external markets. The oil-rich countries of the Middle East are an example. Almost all of their gross national product is exported, and internal demand is satisfied by imports. The economic health of these countries depends entirely on the global demand for their goods. Such a situation is extremely unstable, and these countries make every effort to regulate the global market for oil and oil-based products and to broaden and diversify their economies.

Even those countries that seem to have everything can obtain savings in external markets. You can always find exotic products manufactured in other countries for a lot less money than you can produce them yourself.

External trade was so important for the economy that governments began to take every opportunity to participate actively. Their methods depended on external trade politics that were in many respects defined by the economic power of the state and its general economic policy.

A country's **balance of trade** is dependent on how much it imports and exports. It can be positive or negative. If your exports exceed your imports, you will have a positive balance, and a negative balance if the situation is reversed. If your balance of trade is positive, more money is coming into the country than is going out for purchases from other countries. This is good for your producers and is usually encouraged by the government. There is an exception, however. Let's say that your wheat is in high demand overseas, but there is an unexpected poor harvest and domestic price increases threaten to bring about extreme social unrest. Under these circumstances, the state might introduce a ban on grain exports.

Customs tariffs are the usual means used to regulate external trade. These can take the form of import tariffs that protect domestic producers from competition with cheaper imported goods or export tariffs that help to avoid depleting the domestic market. In either case, the duties collected replenish the state treasury.

Import and export quotas give the government an even tighter control over external markets. Government bureaucrats decide who gets these quotas, and while it is understood that the government treasury will suffer by not getting custom duties, it can be quite lucrative for those who distribute the quotas.

Specific standards can be set for imported goods and prohibitions established for goods that, in the eyes of the state, represent a danger for public health or moral rectitude. Usually the products under strict import control are alcohol (completely banned in some Islamic countries), weapons, narcotics, and pornography. In countries where the state fully regulates the economy, the government maintains the strictest control—a monopoly—on foreign trade.

External trade policies are part of the foreign policy of any government. They can strength relationships with friendly countries and exacerbate animosities with others, hence the term "trade war". There are well-known examples of the establishment of an embargo, or a complete ban on goods from a certain country. Before the apartheid regime was lifted in South Africa, goods from that country were internationally sanctioned. Southern Rhodesia was subjected to such punishment when it promulgated a racist regime and declared independence from England. Economic pressure can be a very effective weapon, especially when the country depends heavily on exports and imports. But it can also be a stimulus for domestic production in the affected countries.

In addition to the export and import of goods, there is also reexport. Take the importer who buys and imports goods into the country but then cannot sell them, or incurs a loss. Then in another country he finds a buyer ready to purchase these goods that then become reexported. They are recorded separately in customs statistics. But in many cases reexport of the imported goods is forbidden by the terms of the initial purchase contract. Why and how should this be the case?

Let's say that you are exporting some sort of goods to country A. You have a long-established business relationship with an importer in this country, and this importer consistently purchases large quantities of your goods. Nevertheless, you advertise in country B and find another buyer who also wants to buy your goods. To gain access to the new market, you have dropped the price below that of country A. So your buyer in country B thinks it would be a good idea to resell those same goods in country A since he can turn a profit by doing so. This disrupts your relationship with your buyer in country A and under-mines your market in that country.

The reverse also can happen. You go into a new market with a high-er price than you have established with previous customers in other countries. These customers can then profitably reexport goods they purchase from you and undermine your position in the new market. Such situations are far from rare. To protect yourself from these kinds of annoyances, you include in your contract a clause that prohibits reexport of your goods.

Money follows goods, so let's see what happens when money goes beyond national boundaries.

International Payments, Currency Rates and Balance of Payments

Let's first recall that in talking about exports and imports, we have so far ignored the service industry. Nevertheless, this also is an item in international trade. What is included in this category that we call "invisible exports"? First, there is transportation of goods. We have already seen that an import price may include the cost of transportation. If the importer purchases goods in another country and arranges to transport them, the cost of transportation is not included in the price. But if the price of goods includes shipping, then this service has been purchased abroad. Even if the buyer hires the transporter in his or her own country for domestic currency, the transporter will incur expenses in the country from which the goods are bought and, in all likelihood, in several countries through which the goods transit. These costs include road and port tolls, purchase of fuel, vehicle repair, registration, crew expenses, etc.

Day and night, vehicles of all sorts move across the surface of the earth: ships, airplanes, automobiles and trains are all busy carrying goods and people. Each category of transportation has its own market, the most significant being marine transport or global freighters. The transportation of goods underwent a technological revolution during the 1970s when the widespread use of containers significantly reduced transshipment costs. Goods could now leave the seller's warehouse and arrive at the purchaser's in a container that simply changed transport vehicles along the way. All the same, the transportation of goods remains a big item in international payments.

Another service that is closely connected with the transportation of goods is insurance. If the buyer acquires goods at the CIF (cost, insurance, and freight) price, then he or she pays for both transportation and insurance for the goods. Who gets this money? The first recipient is the seller, who must turn around and pay for the services of the transporter and the insurance premium.

Insurance costs are the second significant item of "invisible exports" in the international trade of goods. These are also paid by the purchaser, although the insurance companies may be located in a third country. Insurance companies usually reinsure their risk: they break it into smaller pieces and, with an appropriate share of premium for the insurance, sell it to other companies. The principal global market for insurance is in London.

Insurance is not necessarily connected with goods only. You can insure whatever risk you like, from the death of your favorite pet to ocean liner disasters and losses from earthquakes.

People also cross borders for business or pleasure and incur costs in the other country. For some countries, foreign tourism is a significant part of the economy. In resort regions, such as the Caribbean, services connected with foreign tourism can account for up to 90 percent of all the domestic product of these states.

Migrant workers too transfer a sizeable portion of their earnings (about US$400 billion per year) across the borders. In countries such as Bangladesh, the export of their human resources to the oil-producing countries of the Persian Gulf comprises a significant source of income from abroad.

Capital, in addition to goods and people, also crosses international boundaries, but we will look at this movement a bit later.

Both importers and exporters must pay for their transactions. How do they do so? What happens to money that has to be exchanged in the process of international market transactions?

In earlier times merchants would arrive in another country with their goods, sell them for local currency, purchase local goods, take them home, and then sell them for their home currency. For their efforts, the merchants—or commercial guests as they were called—made a good profit. But for that they also took serious risks. Even today, there are companies that do nothing but trade. With the expansion of production, however, producers themselves began to engage in foreign trade. They were thus able to increase their income instead of giving a significant share to the merchants. But this required a means by which money could be converted and transferred from one country to another.

As we saw in the first chapter, at one time, you had to go to the local moneychangers to exchange your government's currency for local and then use it to buy goods. You could even complete the transaction in your own country. The moneychangers would look at your currency and, if it was minted from gold or silver, check the weight and purity (the precious metal content). They would then give you its assessed value in the local currency, not forgetting to deduct the commission. How much would they give you? If the local currency was also minted from gold or silver, the amount would easily be established by calculating the purity and weight of the precious metal content of the coins. If, however, you had some type of banknote or obligation from the bank of your country to accept it as legal tender, the moneychangers would have to determine the reliability of the currency and how attractive it would be to their other clients. They would do this by evaluating the stability of the government that issued the money or the bank that issued the obligation and by calculating the balance between supply of and demand for that currency in their daily transactions. Modern banks do exactly the same thing.

International trade payments begin with establishing the currency of contract price of goods and the currency of payment. If the payment is in the currency of the sellers, the purchasers must buy that currency and pay the sellers. If the payment is in the currency of the purchasers, the sellers, having received their proceeds, must then exchange them for their own currency in order to cover their domestic expenses. Both exchanges carry some risk of loss. As a seller, you would expect to receive some predetermined amount in your own currency; the bank, however, might give you less, citing a fall in the exchange rate. The buyer incurs similar risks.

You can avoid these risks by establishing a third currency that is acceptable to both the buyer and the seller. When the price is established in one currency and the payment in another, there must be agreement on the exchange rate and the date on which the exchange will be made. This also serves to reduce the risk connected with fluctuating rates of exchange. All these terms are negotiable and in many ways depend on the stake each party has in the transaction. Sometimes a currency for the transaction has already been determined by global market practice. For example, the prices for oil and petroleum products, as well as a whole series of other bulk goods, are usually established in US dollars.

The buyer and seller, driven by their respective interests, determine the method of payment. This depends largely on the goods in question and the level of trust between them.

Let's take the simplest of payment methods: encashment. The seller dispatches the product to the purchaser and transmits to his or her bank the documents that transfer the ownership of the goods (an ocean bill of lading if the goods are transported by sea, a waybill or warehouse receipt if the goods are released from a warehouse) with the instruction to give them to the buyer after payment for the goods is received. The seller's bank establishes contact with the buyer's bank, and an agreement is made to transmit the documents to the buyer only after payment has been received from him or her. There is some risk in this arrangement for the seller. The goods are already *en route*, but the money will be received at some unknown point in the future. What if the buyer goes bankrupt during this time? He or she won't receive the goods, but the seller will incur additional costs to have the goods returned.

A letter of credit, an alternate method of settlement, guarantees that the seller will receive payment. To execute a letter of credit, the seller affirms to the buyer that he or she has the goods and is prepared to ship them, then asks that the buyer open a letter of credit, and instructs his or her own bank to complete the transaction. The buyer's bank contacts the seller's bank and establishes the letter of credit in favor of the seller. Once the transportation documents are received at the seller's bank, the money is withdrawn from the letter of credit and put in the seller's account.

The most reliable method by which the seller receives payment is the irrevocable, confirmed letter of credit. It indicates that funds are already in the bank of the seller as confirmed by the bank of the buyer. Neither the buyer nor his or her bank can retract the funds. Even this, however, still does not offer a 100 percent guarantee. The seller may dispatch the goods and go to the bank with his or her irrevocable, confirmed letter of credit in hand only to find that in the meantime the bank has gone bankrupt and closed its doors.

Well, there is never a 100 percent guarantee in the marketplace. You can get counterfeit money as change at a flea market. In ritzier places, a cashier could ring up the same item twice. And we haven't even talked about the quality of goods. In the international marketplace, there are dedicated inspection companies hired to check the goods before shipping to ensure that they meet contract standards. All these risks, however, have not killed the market; in fact it has only expanded, reflecting the development of specialization and cooperation in the global economy.

The easiest and most common practice of payment, is, still, the first method with some (usually thirty days) credit. But it works well only between the parties who have established themselves as reliable partners. That is why business reputation is so important, not only in the domestic market but also, and especially so, in international trade.

For international payments, just like domestic, banks rarely transfer cash to each other. Rather, they open mutual accounts to keep track of who owes whom and how much. The banks also establish among themselves an upper limit of liability for each other. Only when the upper limit is exceeded is the bank required to pay cash. Once again, cash is not often used to settle the debt. If, for example, bank A owes money to bank B, it is most likely that bank B owes money to bank C, which in turn, owes money to bank A. In the contemporary banking system, every major bank holds accounts for other major banks, and mutual offsets almost eliminate the need for cash transfers between banks. A comfortable arrangement indeed! But only until one of the banks, having accumulated a substantial debt to the other participants, suddenly ceases operation. For this reason, in banking relationships, as in the market in general, it is very important to have a good reputation. Sometimes a banker will more readily accept a loss rather than destroy his or her reputation in the business world.

Because the element of trust and reputation are so important, one of the most highly guarded secrets of international banking is the access code or password by which funds are accessed and transactions made. Not many state secrets are as closely guarded as these codes. Special attention is devoted to defending the electronic network that transmits electronic banking transactions. And still, there are successful break-ins by skillful hackers.

From where do banks that are engaged in international payments take the foreign funds needed by their clients? If the bank specializes in import/export services, this is not an issue. Exporters sell their foreign currency earnings to the bank and receive the equivalent in local currency. The bank sells foreign currency for local currency to the importers. But where is the guarantee that the inflow of funds will match the outflow? If you consider that accounts are settled with the currencies of various countries, the chances of these amounts balancing each other is about as small as the world ending tomorrow. The banks can, of course, ask their network banking partners if they have the currency required by the client at any given moment. But this can be an extended search, and in the business world delay means loss. So the country's central bank comes to the rescue. Other banks buy foreign currency from and sell it to the central bank, which establishes the rate at which foreign currency is exchanged for domestic. There are two exchange rates for each currency: the first is the rate at which the bank will buy the currency, and the second, the rate at which it will sell that currency. You can guess which of the two will be higher. If the central bank does not have a sufficient amount of the currency in demand in the country, the bank can buy the required amount from the central bank of the country whose currency it needs or from any bank that has a surplus. Payment can be made in its domestic currency, if there is a demand for it, or in the currency of some third country. In extreme cases, settlement can be made in gold, which is valued universally.

What is the basic benchmark for a foreign currency exchange rate? Why do we say a currency is over- or undervalued? What are we comparing it to besides the rate of, say, three days ago?

The most common standard is purchasing power parity. Let's take one set of goods and services in country A and an equivalent set in country B and then compare the costs in each country's currency. The result of this comparison will be the correlation between the currencies of countries A and B. The development of modern statistics has made this approach very simple.

Much the same analysis can be made for another method of calculation: gold parity. Using this method of comparison, the relationship between the currencies is established by evaluating how much of each currency is required to buy an ounce of gold in the marketplace.

The exchange rate established by these methods, however, is just the beginning; other powerful forces have yet to act on the market—the supply and demand for one currency or another.

If the Bureaus of Customs can give us an exact accounting of the quantities and costs of the country's imports and exports, then the country's central bank collects the data from other banks and can provide the data on the amounts of currency exchanged not only for sales and purchases of goods, but also for the sales and purchases of services. When all payments for the purchases and sales of goods and services are added up, the difference between them is the country's **balance of payments**.

This balance of payments includes the trade balance. It is possible to have a positive trade balance (that is, exports exceed imports) but at the same time to have a negative balance of payments. For example, China and the oil-producing countries of the Middle East each have an enormous positive balance of trade that is almost completely offset by their expenditures on foreign travel and study, overseas investments, and so forth.

But let's return to the question of payments. Offers to purchase or sell foreign currency come in to the country's central bank. The offers come from the banks that are serving their various clients—people exporting goods and selling services to foreign customers, incoming tourists, people holding capital accounts, and others who collect income from foreign capital investments. The demand is created by importers, people traveling abroad for business or pleasure, and people depositing capital in foreign countries. On the basis of this supply and demand, the central bank determines the exchange rates for buying and selling foreign currency.

All this assumes there is no interference by governments; however, they are rarely neutral observers of critical economic processes. In a pure market economy, the central bank uses the supply and demand for foreign currency, and the level of trust in the government issuing the currency, to set the exchange rates. When governments regulate the economy, foreign currency control plays an important part in their economic policies.

When a foreign currency goes up in value or appreciates, one can get more domestic currency by selling that foreign currency. It then becomes advantageous to export goods to the country of that currency. If the exchange rate is going down, it encourages imports since importers have to pay less national currency to buy that foreign currency. This creates an opportunity for the state to influence its foreign trade and payments. The state that controls foreign exchange can even establish different exchange rates for one and the same foreign currency, depending on the nature of the transactions. When the government is in full control of economy, it is usually only the central bank that may possess and trade in foreign currencies and private ownership of them may even be a criminal offense.

Let's say that for some reason demand for our domestic currency abroad begins to rise and, as a result, our central bank's holdings of foreign currencies are also increasing. In this situation, any normal bank would raise the exchange rate for the national currency in order to get a bit more in foreign currencies. If they do this, however, domestic producers and those exporting goods and services will all receive less of the national currency (it is now more expensive) for payments they receive in foreign currency. They pay their workers and other business expenses in their domestic currency, so the fall in the exchange rate obviously affects their income. Prices they charge for exports will have to go up. Thus, their competitive position in the international market diminishes and exports decrease.

Importers of goods and services experience quite the opposite situation. They will need to pay less of their domestic currency to buy foreign currency to support their operations. This is a powerful stimulus for them to increase imports.

The situation reverses when the exchange rate for the national currency falls. Exporters receive more domestic currency for payments they receive in the foreign currency. This is an incentive to grow exports. Conversely, importers must pay more in local currency to get foreign currency and pay for foreign goods. Their income falls.

Those who engage in both imports and exports are caught in the middle. Take the situation where someone imports raw materials, processes them, and exports finished products. For this business, the calculation of profit and loss from the changes in exchange rates gets complicated. It is especially so when the raw materials are imported from one country and the finished product is exported to another. But all of this is just accounting and simply a question of arithmetic. And every businessperson is well aware of any arithmetic that involves income, expenses, and profit.

The fluctuations in exports and imports quickly affect the country's trade balance. We also need to add to this the "invisible" exports and imports; tourists visiting countries abroad are also well aware of which countries they can visit cheaply and which are more expensive. When total payments exceed income, there is a deficit in the balance of payments. That changes the supply of and demand for foreign currency. Left to themselves, market mechanisms will automatically regulate foreign currency rates.

But you hardly ever see that situation. Governments interfere in the process. They defend the interests of the domestic producers, hoping to get a bit more in tax revenue. By the same token, the improvement in the situation of the working class lowers social stress. On the other hand, the taxes that importers pay may also allow more social benefits to be paid by the state. Any government must take all these factors into account.

The situation gets even more complicated because it is not just one government but any number—all governments whose economies are involved in the international marketplace. What is one country's export is another's import, and each government strives to defend the interests of its own taxpayers.

This is only one part of the story of foreign payments and receipts. To this point we have touched only on current payments. There is another important factor influencing the balance of payments. That is the movement of **capital**.

Movement of Capital

History gives us a simple example to study. The British textile companies imported cotton from overseas territories—Egypt, Sudan, India, and America. They manufactured fabrics that were sold throughout Europe. As time passed, the British weavers became aware of the poverty of their circumstances and began to agitate for better living conditions. What could the manufacturers do? Any confrontation, a strike, uprising, or equipment sabotage would mean a decrease in production, the result of which would be a loss in profit. So a sensible society, trying hard to avoid such upheavals, began to regulate working conditions and wage rates, especially since the income from advanced industrial production and trade was large enough to share. What were the unfortunate entrepreneurs to do now? What if the entire operation were to be relocated to a place without an imminent prospect of such conflicts and regulations? The advantages of this relocation would be twofold: first, you could put the squeeze on the wages of the domestic workers since there are fewer positions. Secondly, you could eliminate the cost of transporting the waste inherent in raw cotton. The closer manufacturing is to the place where raw materials are extracted, the lower are the transport expenses and the higher the profits. But the most important factor is the wage that you have to pay to workers hired in the overseas territories.

When raw materials producers were also colonial possessions or dependent territories, such a transfer of production was quite simple. You could take the spinning and weaving machines to the country where the cotton was grown, organize and set up the equipment, train the local artisans, and start the production. You didn't have to pay the local spinners and weavers anywhere near what you would pay their English counterparts. Due to the local climate, culture, and diets, their basic needs were much cheaper—so profits galore!

Or, take for example, the minerals that are so necessary for industrial growth. The "old" world supplies were almost exhausted. But in territories, newly opened by the ubiquitous explorers from the "civilized" world, the supplies were limitless. There was gold, diamonds, copper, bauxite, uranium, tungsten, molybdenum—the whole periodic table! What's more, the local inhabitants were so "undeveloped" that they did not think that someone might own the wealth of mineral resources under their feet. Now was the time to make them conscious of the moral principles of a more "developed" segment of humanity. After all, they would eventually get there themselves. Why not hasten their development into civilization? This development was facilitated by such companies as De Beers, Union Miniere, Anglo-American and Rio Tinto, whose mineral concessions or tenancy included not only the natural resources but even the entire countries that were unfortunate enough to possess them. Mining equipment was dispatched; technicians and engineers were sent along and supported in living conditions that were impossible and undreamed of at home. And the work began.

Raw materials flowed into the "parent company" in the "mother" country, where they were processed and sold to less fortunate businesses. The prices were, of course, "fair market". And the expenses? Transport, maintenance for wear and tear on equipment, personnel— the cost of local personnel being so modest that it was barely worth the calculation—contributions to the budget of the colonial administrations, and a little something to the home legislators and general public to lend an air of legal respectability to this state of affairs. In return, the whole arrangement was amply defended by the legal system, which looked out for the interests of its entrepreneurs and was secured by the local police and military commanded by expatriates.

This arrangement was so enormously profitable that it provided a serious incentive to change ownership of the foreign territories by armed intervention. Some countries' attempts to do so in World Wars I and II were unsuccessful. But other initiatives worked to the advantage of the perpetrators.

With the flow of history, the time arrived for liberation from colonial dependence, and several factors came into play. Because of the Second World War in Europe, the old colonial powers—England, France, Belgium, and Holland—lost their military, political and economic positions. The victor and the up-and-coming economic power, the United States, also wanted access to virtually cost-free natural riches in the colonies. Add to the mix an increasing level of education and self-apprehension among the local elites in the overseas territories. They were employed in local administration and management, and began to reflect on the existing order of things, especially since the advanced foreigners conducted themselves like gods in the overseas lands. The Soviet Union played no small part in decolonization by giving national elites a powerful ideological weapon of anticolonialism and offering the independence movements serious support in terms of arms and military training. As a result, the political map of the world significantly changed in the middle of the twentieth century when more than fifty new nations came into existence.

But let's go back to economics. What happens with goods and money in these movements of capital? Equipment is being taken out of the home country, but it is not being sold and ownership is not changing. So far, no payment is coming to the owner in the country of its origin, yet somehow this movement must be accounted for. Equipment goes through customs like any other export, but what about the money? Money is being taken from the home country and spent for local expenses—construction of production facilities, workers' salaries, purchase of raw materials. These costs of setting up a business abroad are treated as movement of **capital** and constitute a separate part of the balance of payments, a capital export. They are not included in current payments.

When compared to the export of goods, the export of capital is seen as a characteristic of a higher level of economic development.

Between the two groups of entrepreneurs—those who export goods and those who export capital—there is an ongoing battle. Those who export goods try to persuade the government to lower import duties on raw materials and increase duties on imports of finished products that compete with their own production. Capital exporters need something quite different. They need lower import duties for the finished goods they are bringing in from their overseas enterprises and higher import duties on raw materials so that importing them becomes unprofitable.

This conflict in many ways defines the socioeconomic policies of the government. National producers and exporters of finished goods justifiably declare that by fostering local production, they are creating jobs, lowering the unemployment rate, and decreasing the possibility for social unrest. Capital exporters and importers of finished products object, making an equally justifiable case that by transferring production to countries with lower costs, they produce cheaper goods and lower the overall cost of living for a population weary of soaring prices. This, in turn, reduces social tension. Now, environmental concerns and conservation of natural resources have joined the argument. The proponents of capital export and overseas manufacturing contend that these developments improve environmental conditions in their own country. They are, however, conveniently forgetting the fact that we all live on the same planet.

Without embracing the argument of either camp, we can simply observe that competitive industries seek to lower production costs. It is an objective process driven by the market forces that define socioeconomic development.

Governments are usually actively involved in capital movements. In the second half of the twentieth century, state economic aid to countries that had recently gained independence became widespread. Funds given under the rubric of state aid flowed to areas that, while not providing significant profit, nevertheless were necessary for the whole profit-making system to function. Building roads, bridges, and airports nurtured the development of an internal market and increasingly involved large numbers of the local population in the production and consumption of goods. Founding schools, colleges, and universities fostered the growth of professional skills and inculcated in the younger generation a "correct" way of thinking. Organizing healthcare services lowered the mortality rate in the existing and future workforce. Needless to say, the necessary prerequisite for such state aid was the purchase of equipment and employment of specialists from the countries that were providing assistance.

State aid had three components: outright grants, state credit, and state guarantees for capital outlays and commercial credit available to private entrepreneurs. In some cases the conduits for such aid were and still are international organizations like the United Nations, World Food Programme, World Health Organization and others.

State assistance undoubtedly contributed to a better quality of life for indigenous peoples, although the combination of a tribal social structure and an outpouring of vast amounts of wealth (by local standards) led first and foremost to the enrichment of national elites. But that is a separate tale.

Let's look at how the movement of goods and money across national borders has created the modern world economy.

World Economics

Gradually more and more people and nations became involved in the process of producing and moving goods and capital from one country to another.

In all likelihood, modern world economics had fully taken shape by the middle of the twentieth century. It is true, of course, that even before this happened, various countries had economic ties with each other. But inherent in these earlier relationships was a significant noneconomic component that, without exaggeration, may be called "armed robbery". Colonial powers, which possessed superior weapons and military structures, took control of huge tracts of land with their natural and human resources and then governed them for the benefit of their own manufacturers and consumers. Colonial empires arose. They defended their borders not only with weapons but also by various other means, such as customs barriers and currency controls. How did this come about?

Having become entrenched in a certain region (French West and Equatorial Africa, British India, British East Africa, Belgian Congo, the Dutch East Indies, Portuguese Angola, Mozambique, etc.), the colonial powers introduced the duty-free exchange of goods between the "mother" country and the colony. The exact legal status of the colony was unimportant. In British East Africa, for example, Kenya was a colony while Uganda was a protectorate. Tanganyika was seized from Germany as a consequence of the First World War and became a territorial mandate of the League of Nations under the administration of Great Britain. The fundamentals of the system did not change. Goods imported into the colony from every other country were saddled with higher import duties. This made them uncompetitive.

Furthermore, local currencies, introduced by the colonial powers to accommodate domestic markets, could be exchanged freely only for the currency of the mother country—the English pound sterling, French franc, Portuguese peseta, or the Dutch guilder. The exchange rate was fixed, and a means to exchange local currency directly for other currencies simply did not exist. The result was the emergence of currency zones, the most widespread being the British pound sterling and the French franc. It was a simple yet effective method of controlling the economy of a dependent territory. Those ties remained effective for some time, even after the formerly dependent territories won political independence. The objective of economic "independence" followed immediately upon the attainment of political independence because it very quickly became clear to the young state leaders who the real masters in their countries would be if the market and financial affairs continued along the old paths.

The existing order, which was supported by the state pipeline that largely funneled money straight into the pockets of the national leaders, seemed logical and well established. But it made no provision for the emergence of new forces into the global economic and political arena—primarily, the United States of America.

This country had acquired significant amounts of territory by military force (Texas, California and other regions in the west from Mexico) and by purchase (Alaska from Russia, Louisiana from France and so forth). After these acquisitions, it became clear that economic rather than military force was much more profitable for further economic expansion. Maintaining an army in peacetime was an unproductive use of the workforce and simply irrational. But in order to expand the economy globally, it was necessary to tear down the barriers that the old colonial powers had established on the path to a world marketplace. The results of the Second World War, which made the traditional colonial powers economically and politically dependent on the United States, were instrumental in bringing this about. So were the United Nations and a series of other agencies initiated by the United States. It is no accident that one of the five main bodies of the UN was—and to this day remains—the United Nations Trusteeship Council, which was intended to help colonies and dependent territories achieve national independence.

The second power was the Soviet Union, which quickly regenerated its economy shattered by the Second World War. Adhering to the principles of "proletarian internationalism" (which was always very costly in financial terms), the Soviet ruling elite decided that the political and economic separation of the colonial possessions from their masters would serve to weaken global imperialism. Because of its victory in the Second World War, the influence of the Soviet Union grew immeasurably not only among western intellectuals but also among the national elites of the formerly dependent territories.

In the economic sense, the assistance of the USSR to the newly freed countries of Africa, Asia, and Latin America was pretty much exactly what the Soviet official propaganda called "disinterested aid" or aid without any strings attached to it. The only string was that the recipient country proclaim its anti-imperialist aspirations. Grandiose (without exaggeration) economic projects such as the Aswan dam, the Helwan metallurgical plant, and Nag Hamadi aluminum factory in Egypt or Bhilai metallurgical plant in India gave a powerful economic boost to these countries. Economic aid to China was especially substantial since China, of course, was distinguished by its proclaimed intent to build socialism and by its geographic position and large population. The contemporary economic power of China found its beginning in this assistance provided by its northern neighbor even though at the time that neighbor was itself not that prosperous.

The trading ties of the newly independent states with the USSR developed much more modestly. First, the Soviet Union had no need for the raw materials that were the basic exports of the young states. Except for the tropical fruits that appeared on the shelves of Moscow and Leningrad at the time, the USSR was overflowing with a wealth of natural resources. Incidentally, importing "exotic produce" was very helpful for the Soviet state budget. Bought at "global prices" and sold at "domestic prices" that had been established by the State Planning Committee and the Ministry of Finance, they provided a 200-plus percent profit to the state. Among other imported products, it would perhaps seem that Egyptian cotton was valued more for its explosive properties than for its use in bedding, shirts, and towels. Secondly, the Soviet Union simply had not enough consumer goods that could be sold in competition with the West. Thirdly, to be flexible in the market, one needs to have freely convertible money, which was not the case under centrally planned economies. As a result, trade with the young states was conducted through "clearing arrangements"; bilateral exports and imports were balanced up and the central banks of the USSR and its trading partners settled the accounts. Such a system demanded comprehensive state regulation of foreign trade and payments. For the Soviet Union, this was an integral part of its economic system, but in the newly independent states, the state control over economy was not that comprehensive.

The development of a global economy entailed the collapse of the system of colonial domination and required the elimination of national obstructions to the movement of goods and money. This process was especially dynamic in Western Europe where as far back as 1953 a treaty was signed in Rome, which established the European Common Market and eliminated customs barriers between constituent countries. This organization later became the European Economic Community or EEC, which made provision for the free movement of goods, money, and labor. Even more recently, as we know, the process of integration led to the creation of the European Union.

The process of economic integration in Western Europe, like anywhere else, had both objective and subjective roots. Objectively, economic development requires broader markets. It goes without saying that large-scale production in both the industrial and agricultural sectors has lower costs and is more competitive. In addition, the United Sates, while supporting domestic industries and facilitating their transition from war to peace production, used the Marshall Plan to invest enormous sums of money in the reconstruction of a devastated Europe, and encouraged Europeans to cooperate among themselves. Why did the United States do this? Was it to remove sources of future conflict in Europe, where in the course of half a century the two most destructive world wars had originated? Did it represent the need to form a united front against the Soviet forward tank formations in Eastern Europe and East Germany? In any case, in parallel with the economic integration, a military-political union (NATO) was also created.

The Soviet leadership of the time was not caught napping. In the People's Democracies (as the Eastern European countries that had been freed from fascism by Soviet armies were called) the process of integration, as directed by Moscow, also moved forward. The Council for Mutual Economic Assistance (COMECON) was created as early as 1949. The process of political-military cooperation did not lag far behind. In 1955, in response to West Germany joining NATO, the Warsaw Pact was established. The problem of integration in the context of the global socialist system was that the system rested on the principle of state control and regulation of the economy. Market forces were ignored or suppressed. It is not surprising that with the collapse of the centrally controlled economies, their integration also broke down.

Qualitative changes in international payments accompanied the expansion of trade relations. Originally, gold and silver were the common currency for international payments as well as the basis for national coinage: Louis d'or, piaster, escudo, ducat, taler, and so forth. It is interesting that the names of some modern currencies have their origin from those days. Take the English pound sterling. Initially it was just one pound of silver. It was relatively simple to settle international accounts since the pure metal content of the coins was known. But there were two significant disadvantages. First, it was necessary to transport cash to settle accounts, which represented considerable weight and great risk. Even today, treasure hunters raise the riches lost in transport when the forces of nature were doing their worst.

A second disadvantage was that the available quantities of gold and silver were too small to support the rapidly growing volume of international trade. Of course, credit came to the assistance of merchants in individual towns or in a single country. But international credit, just like international trade, carried higher risks. You might sell goods to your foreign purchasers on credit, but then your respective governments unexpectedly declare war on each other.

Gold, which was attractive to everyone, was the all-purpose currency. The supply of that metal, however, was too small to meet the demand for savings, jewelry, and market transactions, so various states began to issue paper money. At first, the paper money of the strongest national economies was inseparable from gold. Banknotes (bank obligations of large denomination) and credit notes (paper money of lesser value) stated that they could be exchanged for gold currency without limit.

When the principle countries of the world issued gold and silver coinage along with paper currency (although paper money won pride of place for ease in marketplace circulation), gold and paper money could be freely exchanged at a fixed rate. Such a system, called the gold standard, was very convenient since it incorporated trust in the currency and made it a reliable means of market circulation and accumulation of wealth, not only at the national but also the international level. Currencies were exchanged simply based on their declared and fixed gold contents. The gold currency standard also set firm limits for the printing of paper currency. This limit was the possession of gold reserves sufficient to satisfy the need for gold and to support the trust in your currency.

To provide for the lowest level of retail activity (the student buying ice cream or the peasant, kerosene), only brass or copper coinage of small denominations was needed. It would be freely exchanged for silver coins and banknotes, and these, in turn, were exchanged for gold coins, and vice versa. All this was accomplished at the face value shown on the coins and banknotes.

This system could, and did work well as long as governments supported the free exchange of their currencies for gold at a fixed rate. Under this regime, it was not necessary to have on hand as much gold as the total value of the brass and silver coins minted and paper money printed. When there is faith in the money, comfort with the use of paper currency, and no inflation, it is necessary to keep only a minimal quantity of gold on hand. This serves primarily to settle external obligations.

There was a danger, however, for a country with big foreign trade deficit. Foreign exporters to that country could accumulate its currency, exchange it at the bank for gold, and take the gold to their own country, thus emptying the depositories of that country's treasury. Under these circumstances, the country buying the goods and services would experience a shortage of gold to spend on imports. This gold shortage would establish the limits for imports, and the situation would be self-correcting. Domestic production (including for export) would become more profitable, thus balancing the country's gold deposits. The system worked if the state did not print excessive paper money.

Everything went along swimmingly. If some country had insufficient gold, the British pound sterling, the primary reserve currency of the nineteenth century, came to the rescue. If your goods and services were selling well on the external market, you could receive in exchange pounds sterling or convert your earnings from the currency you received into pounds sterling, and at a fixed—seemingly once and for all—rate, purchase gold from the Bank of England. But gold was primarily needed by jewelers and dentists. Paper money was much more convenient and safe enough if sufficiently backed by the real production of goods and services that were in demand on the market. Poet Aleksandr Pushkin's well-known hero Eugene Onegin, although a genteel rake, had read the works of Adam Smith, the leading economist of the time, and was able to participate in a serious economic discussion and explain to his listeners how nations could prosper by producing goods instead of hoarding gold.

This whole idyllic age ended in 1914. Global war erupted and with it came the end of the era of the gold-currency standard. To cover military expenditures, the European governments began to print paper money in much larger quantities than were necessary for market circulation. In the meantime, the production of goods and services available on the market was sharply curtailed. Only goods and services destined for military use were increasing. These were incinerated on the fields of battle in Europe where the most productive forces of humanity were devoured by the flames. In these circumstances, even Great Britain (the country on whose possessions the sun never set) could not exchange paper currency for gold at the previously fixed rate of exchange.

At the end of the First World War, the US dollar was starting to take off. Before this, it had generally been a peripheral currency, operating far from the global centers of international business. But behind the dollar stood a healthy economy producing great quantities of goods and services, which were needed in a war-torn Europe experiencing massive social upheaval. Would you like American goods? Be our guest—but we take payment only in dollars. Oh, you don't have dollars? No problem. You can buy them from our central bank (the Federal Reserve). How will you buy them? With gold, of course. It costs only thirty-five dollars per troy ounce (31.1 grams). And so gold flowed into Fort Knox from the whole world, including the Soviet Union, which had just appeared on the global political map. Central banks all over the world began to carry their reserves not only in gold but also in American dollars that were at that time as good as gold.

In the interval between the two world wars, the American dollar put serious competitive pressure on the British pound sterling and became the second currency of international payments. The pound sterling continued to be exchanged for gold at a fixed rate since it relied on the huge resources of the British colonial empire, but this quickly ended. At the height of the economic crisis of 1929–1933, both England and the United States ceased to exchange their currencies for gold at a fixed rate. The United States, however, reestablished this exchange rate in 1934. England and France tried to sustain the credibility of their currencies by resorting to the gold bullion standard. They exchanged their currency for gold at a fixed rate, but the gold was to be in bullion. It was possible to purchase it freely but only if you started with a fairly hefty amount of money. For example, the smallest bar of gold was 12½ kilograms and it cost £1,700. For that money at that time you could buy a Rolls Royce.

The Second World War sorted out the global currencies according to the economic power of the issuing states. In 1944, in Bretton Woods, New Hampshire, an agreement was reached that guaranteed that only one currency would be exchanged for gold at a fixed rate: the US dollar (thirty-five dollars per troy ounce). Other currencies were pegged to the dollar at a fixed rate of exchange that would be maintained by the central banks issuing them. Thus, the gold exchange standard was formally adopted, and with it, the global supremacy of the US dollar was established. The rate of mutual exchange for the remaining currencies was determined by their rate in relation to the US dollar.

Before taking a look at the modern picture of the global currency exchange, let's take a minute to ponder why the main economic players have tried to secure a leading position for their own currency.

In the first place, the state that issues the currency that all the other countries need has little fear of inflation. The United States, let's say, issues dollars to pay the part of its budget not covered by revenue. Part of this money goes for the purchase of goods and services from other countries. But not all of this money returns to the American market to buy American goods and services. Rather, it sits as a financial reserve in the depositories of the central banks of the other countries. The dollar becomes more and more attractive. American banks could lend dollars at a higher rate of interest and, correspondingly, pay a higher rate for deposits, which attracts available money from other countries creating, again, additional demand for dollars.

Secondly, it is more convenient for your foreign payments. If you have established the price of the major goods on the global market in the currency of your own country, your exporters and importers of these goods bear no risk if the exchange rate fluctuates. Such a situation now obtains in the global markets for petroleum and some other bulk commodities, where prices are established in US dollars.

There is still another significant factor. If you plan to invest your money in a foreign business, it is easier to do so in a currency that is accepted the world over. Any additional currency exchange means a loss for you and income for the moneychanger.

We can say with certainty that the leadership of the US dollar is associated with the export of capital from that country.

But the predominant position of a currency conceals some high risks, the most important and tangible being the loss of faith in the currency. This happens when a government, presuming on the attractiveness of its currency, issues it in quantities greater than what the rest of the world needs for the purchase of goods and services and as a reserve.

This is exactly like borrowing money and not repaying it. The minute you decline to repay your debt, no one will extend you another loan. Any currency, of course, is valuable only to the extent that you can buy something for it. Postponing a purchase and keeping foreign currency is meaningful only if the potential buyers believe that tomorrow they can buy no less than they can buy today for the same amount of money.

Just such loss of trust has historically befallen the US dollar. To cover its expenses, the government of the United States issued more dollars than was necessary for the world market. The stockpiles of dollars in the central banks of other countries reached the limits of faith in this currency. The subsequent events played out as you might expect. It is reported that at the beginning of the 1970s, the president of France, Charles de Gaulle, a military general and head of the wartime French Resistance Movement, ordered a plane to be loaded with millions of dollars that had been stockpiled in the central bank of France and sent them to the United States. This was the money that Americans had used in France to buy property on the Cote d'Azur and that American tourists had spent as they flooded into Paris. The general ordered that the money be presented to the American Federal Reserve and exchanged for gold at the official rate of thirty-five dollars per troy ounce. Following this, in 1971, the president of the United States, Richard Nixon, declared that he was suspending the exchange of dollars for gold at the official rate. The era of the gold standard had ended.

From this event—historic from the point of view of international monetary relations—followed a whole series of unilateral and multilateral measures to adjust to a new system of international payments. Without going into detail about each of these, let us note that they led first to the abolition of an officially fixed rate of exchange. A currency was worth only what you could get for it on the open market. This, of course, pertains to a fully convertible currency. The price for gold also began to float freely in the market and recently reached a level unheard of before the abrogation of the gold standard—US$1,400 per troy ounce. The objective laws of economics put everything in its proper place.

Nowadays the US dollar, the euro, the Japanese yen, the British pound sterling, and the Swiss franc are considered primary global currencies. Except for the Swiss franc and the British pound sterling, these currencies reflect the economic position of the countries issuing them (or group of countries, in the case of the euro). The Swiss franc is supported by the sound banking system of the country that, as already noted, renders specific banking services and has large quantities of gold. The British pound sterling is significant because London is a powerful financial and insurance center as well as a global marketplace for nonferrous metals and rubber.

Based on the economic indicators it would seem that the Chinese yuan should be included among the major currencies; the Chinese economy has reached a prominent place in the world, but the yuan is not a freely convertible currency. The government regulates the exchange rate, and the global currency market does not take such currencies seriously. For the free market, any strong interference by a government is a departure from the norm and constitutes an unacceptable risk.

Some other currencies also have international status: the Canadian dollar, the Singapore dollar, the Australian dollar, and the South African rand. But they have their own spheres of activity and are limited to a particular region.

The market is simply the market; anyone can buy and sell. Together with banks, currency speculators are active players in the global currency market. They can be very wealthy individuals or financial companies. When we exchange money for a trip abroad, we essentially also become participants in this market. Within the limits of our personal means, we create demand for one currency and supply of another. But when major players enter the market—not because they want money for travel to France or relaxation in Turkey but because they want to make profits—the currency world holds its collective breath. These players crush "weak" currencies and then scoop them up cheaply to sell or dispose of at a profit. The figures in such operations can run into the hundreds of billions. Even governments are wary of such operations, and their central banks must react promptly to mitigate the possible economic risks.

Let's reduce such market manipulations to their simplest form. Let's pick a currency that is not supported by a robust or fast-growing economy or where the central bank of the country does not have healthy reserves. There are many such countries in the modern world. Using our available cash, we begin to buy up this currency on the foreign exchange market. The market reacts to the increase in demand by increasing the rate of exchange for that currency. The entrepreneurs of that country now have the ability to purchase more goods and services from other countries and deposit their capital there. To do so, they go to their local bank for credit. These banks in turn borrow from the central bank. The interest rate for loans goes up. The country's export market for its goods suffers or is destroyed because its competitiveness on the global market falls—buyers must pay for their goods in the more expensive currency. At just this moment you dump your amassed funds of that currency on the market, which leads to a sharp decrease in its exchange value; there is no demand for such quantities of this currency. Those entrepreneurs who have bought goods and services abroad go bankrupt since they have to pay much more for them in their own, now devalued, currency. The trust on which credit was based has been exhausted. So now is the time to buy for next to nothing the devalued currency and put this money in some kind of income-producing business or real estate in the suffering country. When that happens, the exchange rate begins to rise and we can again sell this currency at a profit. It's all about the choice of target and the right moment to buy and sell. More complicated schemes may include several currencies.

What can the central bank of the target country do to counter such currency piracy? When there is increasing external demand for the national currency, it is necessary to support its supply, even if this means printing additional money while at the same time building up reserves of the incoming "strong" foreign currency. Thus, the central bank will restrain its domestic currency price increases. Then, when large amounts of your currency are dumped on the market, you must purchase them using the accumulated reserves of the foreign currencies. In other words, it is imperative to avoid at all costs sharp jumps in the exchange rate. That's easy to say. But how can anyone predict that one's currency has become the target of massive speculation? For this, the bank must employ qualified economists who watch the smallest changes in the global currency market with an eagle eye.

And how can individual entrepreneurs insure against losses when there are abrupt changes in the exchange rate? You can set the prices for your goods in a "major" currency so when the exchange rate falls, you receive more of the foreign "weak" currency. But this requires agreement with the purchaser. Such issues are the subject of contract negotiation. What if you can't come to terms with the purchaser?

For such a situation, there is something called **hedging**. Let's say that you sell goods abroad, with payment due thirty days later in foreign currency. During this month the value of your currency, which you need to cover your own expenses, might shoot up in relation to the currency of payment, so that you would receive less than you had counted on. To avoid possible losses, you buy your own currency or a "strong" currency at the going rate with payment to be made in your contract currency but only after one month. This arrangement will work if the persons selling the currency you need believe that its value will not change or will fall and they will get their profit.

Clearly, such insurance costs money and makes sense when dealing with large sums. The bank and financial company currency traders turn over billions in such deals during the course of the day. Each one of their decisions, which are made in minutes if not seconds, can result in millions in profit or losses. It's not surprising that the majority of foreign exchange traders swap their job for something more tranquil or, generally, retire early in their careers.

Exporters of goods and services, just like other sellers, seek to maximize the amount of money they will receive. If they establish a price and receive payment in foreign currency, there is a risk that when it comes time for payment, they have less to put in their bank account than they had planned on. This happens if the price for their currency goes up. But the currency might fall, and then they would receive more of it. In the case of falling domestic currency, exporters are encouraged and importers who have to pay more to buy foreign currencies are at a disadvantage. This phenomenon opens doors to currency rates manipulation and even "currency wars".

The euro as an international currency is an interesting experiment. With a successfully functioning European Economic Union as the basis, the euro was introduced in 1999 as a common accounting currency for the participating countries. Then, in 2002, the euro became the only currency in circulation in seventeen European countries with 320 million people, and their national currencies disappeared. In 2006, there were 620 billion euros circulating globally. This was more than the number of US dollars! One must keep in mind, of course, that a significant part of retail purchases in the United States are done through the credit card system without using cash.

The advantages of a single currency are obvious. You remove all exchange rate risks when entrepreneurs in different countries do business with each other. You eliminate bank commission on the exchange from one currency to another. The common market becomes truly common and extends to its participants greater opportunities to expand the production of goods and services.

There is yet another point of fundamental importance. We have determined that with some exceptions issuing money was always the function of the state. The national rulers minted or printed money to strengthen the national economy and ensure political stability or to attain their own goals. With the euro, the situation has changed dramatically. This currency is issued by the European central banking system, and monetary policies are laid out by the European central bank. In other words, the economic independence of the national governments has been significantly limited. Member countries of the euro system must maintain a certain level of economic stability; otherwise, the exchange rate for the euro on the international market might suffer and the system would collapse. National governments must not permit budget deficits or growth of state debt beyond established limits. The recent financial problems in Greece and several other countries of the European Union were linked to just this problem—the level of public debt turned out to be higher than the government would admit and exceeded established limits.

The power of national governments has always been limited by the country's boundaries. Beyond its borders, the state encounters forces of the same order and over which it has no authority. On the other hand, economic laws have no borders. Governments can stimulate or restrain economic activity within their borders, but beyond the borders, the measures taken by other states apply. For centuries, this collision spilled over into bloody conflicts, but this situation has changed in our time.

What have we established thus far?

National and even individual economic processes are essentially the same as global economic processes. The demand for and production of goods and services are universal in character. If the separate actors—a family, entrepreneurs, companies, or countries as a whole—produce and sell more goods and services than they consume, they will have savings or free financial resources and will try to invest them safely and profitably. In the opposite situation, when consumption exceeds production and sales, the need to borrow money becomes unavoidable. But borrowing comes at a price, a price that is dependent on such factors as trust, risk, and the general economic situation. Increased consumption on credit may surpass limits beyond which trust is lost and credit is no longer available. Then it becomes necessary to rein in consumption or spend the accumulated savings or sell assets, or all three. Just as this is a painful process for an individual or a family, it is also painful at the national level.

Globalization

The laws of economics break down national boundaries. Culture and tradition follow goods, services and capital across the borders, and, in their turn, create additional demand for "overseas curiosities". An economically strong state—that is, a nation with a high level of productivity and output of goods and services that are in high demand—wins newer and newer markets. Other nations may try to counteract this pressure, and if their economies are strong enough, they will be successful for a time. The foreign markets, however, have huge advantages. If your country produces goods or services at the lowest unit cost, then an increasing number of markets will be open to them. Product lines will grow, employment will rise, and profits will increase. More tax revenue will come into the state treasury. More foreign currency earnings will enable your importers to buy goods that are produced more cheaply in other countries. Consumers—you and I—are the winners.

If you want to sell your goods and services freely in the global marketplace, you will have to guarantee free access to your domestic market for imported goods and services. For many, many years, customs and other types of barriers were the subject of disputes, even wars, and agreements between different countries and groups of countries. Disputes continue even today but on a smaller scale and in more civilized forms. The World Trade Organization (WTO) was established at the end of the twentieth century, and almost all states joined. The organization ensures that barriers to trade are minimized and resolves trade disputes between countries. The global market for goods and services has become just that—global.

The creation of a universal system of information and communication (the Internet) had a stunning effect on the globalization of world markets. Now, with the trust of a bank in the form of a credit card, you can order and receive almost any sort of goods and services from any place on earth. With this capability, you will, of course, choose the cheaper, higher quality goods, thus encouraging the most successful producers—that is, those who produce quality merchandise at the lowest cost. Well, who wouldn't be satisfied with such a system?

As it turns out, there are quite a few unhappy people. They demonstrate outside the venues where world leaders discuss the problems of globalization. Let's see who is participating in these demonstrations. The largest category consists of those who have lost their jobs because production has been transferred from a country with high manufacturing expenses to ones with lower costs. Workers in the industrial countries of Western Europe and North America had mostly joined trade unions. On behalf of their membership, trade unions make agreements with industrialists; one of the major points is the rate of pay (usually an hourly rate). It is the cost of labor that is the primary component of the cost of most goods and services. In developed countries (once again with trade union pressure), a legal minimum wage for all workers has been established. Although the law is often violated, in general, the interests of workers are sufficiently protected. Wages and pay scales are established based on required qualifications and the cost of living in the country. Why the governments of developed countries go to such lengths to defend the interests of wage laborers is another question. Here the preservation of social stability is the main issue. The result, however, is that the cost of the labor force in developed countries is incomparably higher than in countries with lower levels of development and unionization. Climate, culture, and even religious conditions have a role to play in this. But, as we already noted, capital will shift production to where the cost of production is lowest. Thus, workers in the countries of Western Europe and North America become unemployed. Some can perhaps retrain in a new profession that is still in demand in the local market, but for workers of a certain age, this will be difficult to do—and it costs money. It is easier to blame globalization for everything. Trade unionists have been particularly active in such protests because more than anyone else, they have lost out to globalization. With unemployed members, the trade unions cannot collect the membership dues that pay the salaries of the union leaders.

Young people are another category—not only young hoodlums who are itching for a fight with police—but also those who have finished college and are not able to find work commensurate with their training. Or perhaps their chosen specialty is among those goods and services that have been transferred to a country with a lower cost of production. Or perhaps immigrants from developing countries who came in for their studies are ready to work for a lower wage in order to stay in the country where they received their training. To return to the country of their birth with a western education would seem ridiculous. They can work in the same western companies for a lower rate of pay and still support a large family back home. Furthermore, as graduates of western universities, the cultural traditions they have absorbed during their time of study would make them feel like foreigners in their home countries.

In these protests, we will also find activists of the "green" movement or those struggling for a clean environment. They correctly believe that globalization opens a path for polluting manufacturing plants to be transferred to countries with weaker environment protection. For industrialists this is preferable to spending money on treatment of their poisonous industrial waste. Insofar as we have only one planet for everyone, the damage inflicted on the atmosphere, the water, and the flora and fauna has no national boundaries. So issues of the environment should be addressed globally. But most governments in their pursuit of competitiveness of their industries fail, jointly or individually, to address this problem.

Well, it doesn't matter how much demonstrators rant and rave, globalization will grow and spread. Capital gravitates to where it can produce more profit. Goods, services, labor, money, traditions, and culture are migrating across the globe. In the stores of New York, you can buy fish caught in Lake Victoria in East Africa or lamb that roamed the pastures of New Zealand. During the tourist season, waiters—students from Russia, Albania, and Macedonia—work in restaurants in the resort towns of Western Europe and the United States. The service staff in the hotels of the Persian Gulf countries come from Bangladesh and the Philippines. On construction sites in Moscow and London, you can see workers from Moldova, Ukraine, Belarus, and Brazil. An overwhelming number of the consumer goods sold worldwide are made in China. Containerization, the Internet and wireless communications have accelerated globalization. You can book a New York-to-Tokyo flight, and the operator preparing the ticket might be located in Calcutta or Bombay. If you were to write a detective novel or a textbook on economics, you could publish it yourself and sell it globally on the Internet. Moral codes and principles of social organization that have developed in one civilization have become the property of all humanity and, if they seem attractive enough, can lead even to political changes.

Governments that are unsure of the competitiveness of their entrepreneurs and of the support of their people feverishly search for a means to control the general movement of goods, services, capital, and information. Above all, governments are troubled by the movement of ideas if those ideas do not conform to the governing principles of the country. For a time they may succeed in exerting control. But historically, sooner or later, globalization will overcome national boundaries. What does this mean for human society? Many of us (especially those who are a bit younger) will see the impact in our own experiences. Most importantly, though, is to avoid escalation of inevitable frictions that accompany any development of a global magnitude into military conflicts.

Economics and War

In human history, it would be hard to find even one war that did not have economic roots. Wars have been waged to seize slaves, to acquire treasure or fertile and mineral-rich lands, or for easier routes to new sources of wealth. Ideologues and propagandists throughout time invented justifications for wars, but the goal of all wars of aggression was to acquire something of material value. Limited by their agendas, the national leaders, however, often ignored the costs of preparing for and conducting the war, the results of which they could not always accurately foresee.

One could argue that in recent history only the Soviet incursion into Afghanistan was not undertaken for economic reasons. On the other hand, this action was not planned as a war. The leaders of the USSR presumed that this adventure would be limited to a task force of the Ministry of Internal Affairs replacing the Afghan leadership. Citizens of the former Soviet Union know very well where this blunder has led and how it has affected their lives.

Let's take a look at ancient history. Interrelations between various tribes did not always consist of a peaceful exchange of goods. Some clans and tribes would have to change their place of residence and trespass on land that other clans considered their home. Conflicts flared up for other reasons: beautiful young women, the results of a sporting competition and arguments over the exchange of goods. Even simple misunderstandings over differences of language and traditions could escalate into hostility. When this led to a physical conflict, at first all members of the tribe or clan were involved. Over time, it became clear that in such situations those members of the community who were better with fists, cudgels, axes, spears, etc. were more suited for a military career than for any other walk of life. As society developed and specialized trades appeared, so too did a professional military meant to serve as a defensive or attack force.

The development of military skills is a subsection of global history. Let's note only that there are both external and internal reasons for a nation to arm part of its population. Once, anyone who had the ability to collect tribute, levies, and taxes was considered a ruler. In exchange for that collection, the ruler had to guarantee that no one else would try to collect them. In effect, this established the economic boundaries of the ruled land. If the people decided that a neighboring ruler collected fees that were a bit lower, the boundaries could change. Understandably, such events would lead to an armed conflict. Incidentally, even in our own time, such is the nature of conflicts between criminal street gangs.

Well, how does the development and use of the military element in society affect the economy? Let's begin in a time of peace. Most states by various means had managed to persuade their citizens that an army—that is, a special group of people who are always prepared to engage in an armed conflict with others like themselves—was necessary. The strongest part of the argument was this: if the people refuse to feed their own army, they will be forced to feed someone else's army. The only need for an army stems from the assumption that everyone else already has one. Putting aside the logical foundation of such an argument, historically it was reinforced by real events. Let's see what would happen as a result.

Part of society's production of goods and services is withdrawn from the market and consumption. Smelted metals, woven fabrics, and synthetic plastics (especially those of the highest quality) are used for tanks, cannons, rockets, airplanes, cruisers, submarines, bombers, machine guns, automatic weapons, ammunition, mines, military uniforms, and so forth. These products are used even in peacetime, of course. Tanks, airplanes, and other military machinery wear out during military exercises. Cartridges and bullets are used up on firing ranges. But most of these items are stored idly in arsenals and munition depots. And thank God for this!

Workers and engineers who are employed in the production of military equipment get their wages. Usually these wages are higher than in other branches of industry. Thus, the amount of money in the hands of consumers is increasing, but the quantity of goods and services available for sale is not keeping pace. No one (thank God again!) is selling the people rockets, bombers, or tanks. Well, very few people need them. (We are going to talk a bit about international armaments sales further on.)

But this is not the end of the story. The most important resources—people in their prime years and at the top of their game professionally—are taken out of the productive sphere of society. Instead of producing the goods and service needed by other members of society, they are chasing about in forests and fields, in the heavens and under the seas on military exercises, sitting at military headquarters, and devising cunning missions against supposed evildoers, or supporting all of this activity ideologically, judicially, and medically. All of these people are well paid, get healthcare and good pensions that they can benefit from earlier than the rest of the population, and have other benefits. All of them have to be fed (history abounds with examples of the consequences of a hungry army), clothed, shod, and housed, and have to have their laundry done, be given haircuts and medical treatment, and be transported from place to place. The rest of the members of society pay for all of this and in exchange get the military might of their nation.

We saw at the very beginning of the book where this leads: inflation that causes prices to rise. Manufactured goods, raw materials, and fuel that go to the military do not find their way into the general consumer market; this also contributes to price increases. There are fewer goods on the market and more buyers with money. From the point of economics, this is some kind of voluntary madness, wouldn't you say?

Of course, there are some general benefits to the army's existence. First, huge sums of money are spent on the development of new military technologies. And this, like it or not, leads to all sorts of technical innovation and even scientific discoveries that sooner or later make their way to consumers outside military limits.

Besides this, the state has at its disposal a force always prepared for quick action. It is ready to be deployed in any natural disaster or extraordinary manmade situation from floods and earthquakes to mass social unrest. This preparedness can mitigate the economic consequences of such events.

We should also keep in mind that the army attracts to its ranks people, who from youth prefer an active and adventurous lifestyle in the open air to poring over books or studying music or foreign languages. Who knows what would happen to their unbridled energy if the army did not give them the opportunity of personal fulfillment within the framework of strict discipline and subordination?

Overall, however, military expenses are a heavy burden for the normal economy.

International markets offer states with a well-developed military-industrial complex a chance to ease these burdensome consequences. It is a fact that any state power, regardless of size, must have the means to defend itself and maintain public order, and weapons are the means to do so. Clearly, these need to be in the right hands, but that is another question. The state that does not produce its own armaments and ammunition looks for sources from which to obtain them. This creates a legitimate global arms market.

The global arms market is considerably different from the global market for peaceful goods and services. In the first place, it is strictly regulated. The trade laws of a majority of countries require a state license to import and export weapons. You can see why: somebody sells weapons to a neighboring country and then that country decides to make a serious claim, let's say, against your territorial integrity—or if not yours, that of your ally. Well, who needs that? The sale of weapons is always a foreign policy issue for the seller. The UN Security Council regularly introduces a ban (embargo) on the sale of weapons to one country or another, or to an organization, and all countries that are members of the UN must observe the ban.

Regulatory agencies stipulate ways of identifying goods, and in the case of weapons, this is achieved by detailed labeling.

We should immediately note that where there is strict control, there are ways of evading it. Frederick Forsythe, in his book *The Dogs of War*, describes in detail a very simple way to do this. A team of mercenaries is engaged to overthrow the government of some African nation. The leader of this group finds a country that has the weapons he needs and that does not have broad foreign policy interests. Government employees of another country are prepared to represent themselves as legitimate purchasers for a certain consideration. The contract is signed using the services of a company that specializes in acting as an intermediary. The weapons are dispatched to the country of the purchaser as designated in the contract. During the voyage, the captain of the ship that has been hired by the intermediary firm receives orders to change the landing port to the one in the country where the coup is being planned. There the weapons are unpacked and used as designated. Clearly all these maneuvers are accompanied by set payments for silence and assistance in the operations.

Globally, there are quite a few governments ready to sell arms to whomever. There are even countries that can purchase them purportedly for their own needs and then profitably resell them to another buyer without informing the country of origin. Should the weapons then turn up in a completely different state, one can always explain this by saying that they were stolen from the warehouse. "The guard fell asleep, you know, and missed the theft. Can happen anywhere. Our apologies. The guilty parties will be severely punished." Intermediaries play a large role in this trade. They can always cover up any incident in which the weapons fall into the wrong hands. Keep in mind that the arms market is considered more profitable than the trade in illicit drugs. For that reason, there are quite a few people who want to circumvent the regulatory agencies or an international embargo.

Of course, this all relates to small arms: pistols, rifles, submachine guns, and machine guns. And perhaps also mortars and recoilless cannons. More substantive weaponry—tanks, airplanes, artillery, helicopters, infantry fighting vehicles, rockets, submarines, aircraft carriers, and nuclear technology—usually enters the market at the state level. In the last years of the Soviet Union, however, a cooperative agency tried to export modern tanks to some other party. But that was an exception, or, maybe, just one example that the ubiquitous press made public. Still, a nuclear scientist from Pakistan, sold atomic bomb technology to anyone who wanted it, although his shop was also quickly closed.

From the point of view of the government of the arms-producing country, selling armaments is particularly useful for the economy. Judge for yourself: The weapons have already been manufactured and are sitting in the warehouse awaiting the beginning of military action. The nation has already paid for their production from its budget and now can get the money back at the expense of another country that buys the weapons. For countries with a developed military-industrial complex, the export of weapons to foreign buyers has become a perennial source of foreign currency. Sometimes a state with a strong military industry and extensive international interests sells its military wares with the assistance of state credit. How this credit is repaid is a rather delicate question. We know that a significant amount of state credit offered to a number of Arab, African, and Latin American countries to purchase weapons from the Soviet Union had to be written off. If there was any advantage to the seller from such a courtesy, it all related to foreign policy. In this sphere, it is difficult to calculate the economic effectiveness of commercial transactions.

Anyway, all these economic losses associated with arming and supporting the military at a time of peace pale in comparison with those experienced at times of military conflict. Along with the loss of military materiel, the economic potential of the conflict area suffers massive destruction. Yet even this cannot compare with the loss of the most important productive force of the society: its people. While it is difficult to ignore the moral and psychological consequences of mass and unpunished murder, we are dealing only with its economic impact. In addition to the unrecoverable losses of human potential to produce the goods and services needed by society, there remains the issue of paying the cost of caring for the wounds and psychological trauma of the military veterans. We must add to this the greater costs of maintaining law and order since those who are now accustomed to shooting and killing may decide that the members of society who had been spared the massacre owe them more than just some veteran's benefits.

Some economists, however, point to the incontrovertible fact that the wartime destruction of the old industrial capacity and infrastructure leads to a fundamental rebuilding after the end of military action. This is a powerful stimulant for growth in productivity. There are other theories that also find positive elements, including economic, to military conflict. To me, this is wrong! The ideal world would not have armies and the military industrial complexes. Unfortunately, we live in a world that is far from the ideal. So, if the political gurus are correct in thinking that paying for a powerful army equipped with the latest weaponry is a factor in reducing the probability of significant armed conflict, then by all means let us pay the cost. As the ancient Romans said, *Si vis pacem—para bellum* ("If you want peace, prepare for war"). Hopefully, future generations will prove this saying wrong.

Political Economy

Conceptually, this chapter should be the first one. But arguably it is the most tedious since we are going to speak about things that bear little relationship to real life. So prepare yourself to deal with rather abstract concepts.

There are a lot of economic and political-economic theories, so let's start by stipulating that economic theories are concerned only with economic laws and phenomena. Political economy considers how these economic phenomena affect state power and vice versa. There are other branches of economics—for example, the history of economics, economic psychology, finance, economic statistics—but they are of only secondary interest to us now.

Karl Marx was, perhaps, the most popular political economist of the past century and a half. Although Marxism, like any other scientific theory, had and still has its detractors who oppose, refine, and supplement it, a number of its basic points remain valid. What thoughts did Marx most fully set out in his three-volume work *Das Kapital*?

Perhaps the most important aspect of Marx's theory is his study of value added. Building on the works of Scottish economist Adam Smith (the same Adam Smith whose books were read by Pushkin's Eugene Onegin), Marx found that human labor has a dual nature: actual labor and abstract labor. These are simply two sides of the same process. Actual labor creates the consumer value of goods—that is, their concrete benefit. I can sit on a chair; I can wear shoes. Abstract labor creates the value of a product or its ability to exchange for other goods in certain proportions. There is an immediate caveat: the value of a product, although it may serve as the basis of its price, almost always differs, sometimes significantly, from the price.

The value of a product includes the value of the raw materials used in production (boards and nails for chairs, leather and glue for footwear), the cost of wear and tear (depreciation) on the tools used in the production process (saw, hammer, awl), and the labor costs. The cost of labor also includes the means by which the worker supports and reproduces himself (rearing a family if he is not single). A significant component of the labor cost is the cost of acquiring the necessary work skills.

In the process of labor, the worker creates **value added**. Value added is the value in excess of the value of the various components used in production. Once again, we must stipulate that we are talking about value and not about prices.

Value and value added are highly abstract concepts, and unlike prices, they cannot be seen or calculated. Even if workers add up their own costs in making the products (what was spent to produce a chair or a pair of boots), they would have no idea of the value of these items. They would not know the exact value of the goods they have produced until these goods enter the market to be exchanged for other products. There, a comparison of the value of various products will take place through their prices. As we have already established, prices can differ significantly from values. This can happen for a variety of reasons, but the basic one is the balance between supply and demand.

We must immediately qualify this statement: when we are talking about the cost of goods and services we mean the average cost for a category of products. But average data are abstractions. The average temperature in a hospital, as we have already noted, can signify the grave condition of some patients and the eternal peace of others in the hospital morgue. So it is with economics. One producer may have a net cost of production that is lower than an average, and he makes a profit and prospers; another, encumbered by a large family and high expenses for materials, rent and other costs, scrapes by on bread and water. Producers who have the smallest expenses will always push less successful producers from the marketplace. The main factor here is workforce productivity or the quantity of goods produced per unit of time, although there are other qualitative factors.

It is interesting that classical Marxism speaks primarily about goods, but we understand that its statements apply to services as well.

To make the abstract concepts of value and value added clearer, we can compare them with gravity. Nobody sees it, but its forces are always in action. Without them life on earth would be highly uncomfortable if possible at all. Yes, we can measure gravity by weighing ourselves and other things and compare the masses, but it is our invented scale that we use for that.

Regardless of the abstractness of the concepts of value and value added, these measures of human labor are the foundation of the whole process of production and distribution of goods. What's more, value added is the primary source of the development of all human civilization. If there were no surplus in the value of produced goods and services in comparison to the materials used and labor expended in production, well, progress would simply not occur.

There is another interesting aspect to Marx's economic theory. All goods are divided into two very general categories: the means of production and consumer goods. Means of production include the tools of labor—instruments, machinery and other equipment both industrial and agricultural. Consumer goods include everything that humans use up: raw materials, food, clothing, footwear, and so forth. So that production can expand, there must be a certain ratio between production of the means of production and goods for consumption. Marx established this ratio using a simple mathematical formula, which, I believe, was the first introduction of math into the science of economics.

We will not go into all the theses of the three volumes of *Das Kapital* that analyzed in detail such topics as profit, land rent, and interest. Let's look at how in the theory of Karl Marx and his friend, associate, and sponsor Friedrich Engels (himself a successful capitalist) economic questions are associated with political ones—that is, with questions of power. At this point, economic theory becomes political economy and finds its way into political parties' programs.

In human society, those who produce goods enter into a particular relationship with the means of production. Let's take a carpenter. He picks up a saw, a hammer, boards, and nails, and makes a chair. Invisible in the process of the actual labor, but very important for political economy and equally so in real life, is the economic relationship of the carpenter to his tools. This relationship is called the ownership of the means of production. Understandably, if the carpenter owns his own tools and materials, he would be the owner of the final product, the chair. On the other hand, if the owner of the equipment and supplies is someone else, then that person is the one who owns the chair and pays the carpenter an agreed-upon wage for his labor. Relationships that form in the production and marketing of goods and services are called **productive relationships**. From the point of view of political economy, the most important aspect of industrial relationships is that of the producer and the means of production. The linkage of the means of production and production relationships is called **the mode of production**.

Marxist political economy divides all of human history into several epochs that are characterized by which mode of production predominates at any given time. These epochs and how they differ from each other are:

- Primitive communal structure

- Slavery

- Feudalism

- Capitalism

- Socialism

- Communism

- ?

In a primitive communal society, the tribe or clan collectively owns the basic labor equipment. All able-bodied members of the clan work and divide the products of labor equitably or, more likely, as needs dictate.

In a slave-holding society, both labor and equipment are the private property of the slave owners who decide how to distribute the products of labor.

Under feudalism, the lord of the manor owns the basic means of production (the land), but the workers no longer are fully the property of the landowner and can own their own tools. Allocation of the products of labor is partially determined with the participation of the producers.

Under capitalism, the means of production are private property, but workers are free, and contracts with the owners of the means of production determine their share in the products of their labor.

Under socialism, the means of production are common property, and the products of labor are distributed according to the productive contribution of each member of the society.

Under communism, the means of production are common property, and manufactured products are distributed according to the needs of each member of the society.

It's difficult to see what will come after communism, but human society will never stop developing.

An immediate qualification is necessary: not one of the past epochs existed in a pure form. In the primitive-communal structure, some types of tools might have been privately owned by those who best knew how to use them. The tribal patriarch most likely had greater authority over the decisions about who participated in what kind of work and who could claim what share of the goods produced. Under both a slave-holding system and feudalism, there were free artisans who owned their own means of production and freely controlled the goods they produced. Capitalism has a place for a partial socialization of the means of production and allocation of products of labor in accordance with the investment that members of the society make in their production. Under capitalism, some of the products can be distributed according to the needs of society members irrespective of their contribution to production.

In other words, in every era there are elements of the preceding one, and in each, elements of the next era are germinating. In determining a classification, it is important to consider which elements predominate. Even in our own time, there are places where primitive-communal societies still exist. And there are places today where, despite general condemnation, we find elements of slavery.

The transition from lower to higher social formations is characterized by higher productivity of labor. It is fair to say that labor productivity is a decisive factor in the victory of one epoch over the other. Higher labor productivity creates more value and more value added. That means that society, as a whole, acquires more profit. Then it can spend more money on "non-productive" items: science, general education, arts and services. That makes this society more convenient to live in and more attractive to everybody (with rare exceptions) who are in contact with it. What is also important is that the society with the higher workforce productivity can allot more money to build its military might and use it to promote its ideas, norms and economical interests around the globe.

There are yet other methods of classifying different stages of human social development. One analyzes the history of civilization as the transition from hunter-gatherers to an agrarian economy to an industrial one. Following this classification, we now find ourselves in a post-industrial state of development.

Another more general approach maintains that humanity developed from savagery to barbarity and then to civilization. This does not contradict other approaches to classification.

The history of civilization can be analyzed as a function of the organization of production. In this case, development proceeds from the lowest level of production in which there is almost a total absence of the division of labor (every member of the tribe participates in almost all production processes) to the highest form of mass production with very narrow specialization of individual workers (for example, an assembly worker assigned to tightening the screws on car wheels as the car passes on a conveyor belt). The development of specializations and division of labor leads to a higher organization of industry and the concentration of workers in centers of mass production. Dividing production into separate simple operations enables the development of mechanization—the replacement of manual labor by a more productive one, a machine. Industrial development went from artisans' small workshops with crude equipment to factories and mills with machinery and power plants. Increased productivity was a powerful motivating factor in this development from lower to higher levels of specialization. As we saw, the higher the productivity, the higher the amount of surplus goods and, correspondingly, the higher the surplus value and the greater the profit.

A simple example will demonstrate how specialization led to the growth of productivity. Our carpenter, an artisan working alone, cuts a board into pieces to make a chair. Then he puts aside the saw, selects the nails, takes the hammer, and having dovetailed the pieces, assembles and glues them together. Let's divide this process into its component parts and direct one worker to saw the pieces, a second to assemble and fit them, and a third to finish the chair. We see that no time is wasted by leaving the saw to search for a hammer and nails. By the same token, the human body, having become accustomed to one piece of the operation, adapts to make it better and faster. The production of chairs grows not by three times (the number of workers doing the job) but by more than three. It is this additional increment that constitutes the growth in productivity.

But specialization and division of labor have their own adverse aspects. Workers performing simple repetitive tasks lose the ability to develop their talents and, simply put, stagnate. For their employer that is perhaps a good thing, but for the workers themselves, this is degrading.

The transition from feudalism to capitalism marked an industrial transition from the artisan's workshop to the factory with its higher specialization, division of labor, and greater productivity.

Marxism established that while industrial relationships can encourage the development of productive power, they can also hinder this process. For example, slavery produced no impetus for increasing the productivity of the slaves. However much you produced, the owner would give you exactly the same share of the soup. Why exert yourself to avoid the lash of the overseer when the appearance of doing so would suffice? Furthermore, limited consumption constrained production; the slaves, or the majority of potential consumers, had to be content with their meager supplies.

This is exactly how feudalism hindered the development of industry. Industrial development demanded a large number of hired workers, but the potential labor force was occupied in unproductive agriculture where the local feudal lord did everything to ensure that the local peasants retained the least possible number of surplus goods. The income of most of the population was limited as was the market for an array of industrial products.

Marxism divides human society into classes, depending on their relationship to the means of production. In capitalism, there are two main classes: the capitalists (the owners of the means of production) and the proletariat (hired laborers). All the remaining population groups were identified as a social stratum. This concept of classes put an end to the pure science of economics and initiated the concept of political economy.

Marx and Engels, in their comparatively short document *The Communist Manifesto*, concisely and accessibly laid out their major ideas. If you have the time and desire, read a bit of it. It is a very insightful document for its time.

Marxists think that the whole history of human development is a history of class warfare. Simply put, those who own nothing want to acquire something as quickly as possible, and those who have possessions do not want to part with them. Insofar as property owners have material resources under their control, they create the structure that helps them keep their possessions. The state is such a structure. You can read a more detailed account in Engels's popular brochure *The Origin of the Family, Private Property, and the State*.

Marxism divides the organization of human society into two fundamental components: basis and superstructure. The productive power of labor and the production relationships that belong to any given era constitute the basis; all other aspects of social life belong to the superstructure—ideology and religion (or absence thereof), culture, art, political parties and ideas, moral codes, and government organization. The basis and the superstructure are mutually influential, but the basis, as its name implies, is definitive.

According to Marxists, the contradiction between the development of productive power and the productive relationships that constrain this development spills over into conflict between the basis and the superstructure. From within the superstructure, elements that understand the conflict emerge and offer an approach to its resolution. Depending on the severity of the contradiction, the conflict may be resolved by evolution, reform or revolution. The latter would mean a radical destruction of the old productive relationships and the associated parts of the superstructure. The choice of reform or revolution is determined by many historical, ethnic and economic factors. Experience has shown that revolution is the quickest, most drastic way of aligning productive relationships with productive forces. But this is also the most socially painful one.

Marxism is not limited to pure theory. It suggests a concrete path to overcoming the contradiction between the development of productive power and the evolution of productive relationships (private ownership of the means of production) that constrains that development. Because the owners of the means of production do not renounce this ownership voluntarily, orthodox Marxist scholars believe that the only course of action is proletarian revolution—that is, forcible expropriation and complete replacement of a state system that always defends the interests of the ruling class. At this point Marxism and its followers become the worst enemy of the society that is based on the private ownership of the means of production.

Some reservations are immediately called for. There are other theories that elucidate the conditions and development of human society. For example, one theory claims that development is just the result of human psychology. Another theory states that, in general, all development of civilization is programmed and directed by forces outside of human reason and beyond human comprehension. In my view, Marxist theory is the most elegant and consistent, but it is a matter of taste.

The theoretical foundation of Marxism in general has never been refuted. There are, however, some doubts about its details—for instance, the conclusion that the general rate of return tends to fall. If this is true, what are the limits of this decline? And what becomes of the surplus goods that form the basis of value added and profit? Or the statement about the ultimate impoverishment of the working class under a capitalist system? These theoretical conclusions have yet to be supported by practice, and practice is the main indicator of the validity of any theory.

We must qualify the analysis by saying that Marx constructed his theory by examining capitalism in the beginning stages of its development. In Russia, Lenin's attempts to amplify Marx's theory with the doctrine of imperialism as the final stage of capitalism have not been borne out to this stage of development. Perhaps that is for the best. In any case, the development of human society is a process far more complicated than can be described using only economic and socioeconomic categories. People's ideas and emotions play an active role in this development. As technology develops, especially in communications, more and more people are drawn into the process of management of their society. People will decide what human society will look like in the future. These decisions will, hopefully, rely on knowledge of the objective laws of development, including the laws of economics.

Have you actually managed to read this far? Your patience is commendable and should be rewarded. The author praises your stubborn and tireless pursuit of knowledge. Your reward is your familiarity with the field of economics, although your knowledge of it has only just begun.

Glossary

Balance of payments—the difference between payments coming into the country and disbursements leaving it.

Balance of trade—the difference between a country's exports and imports.

Bankruptcy—the declared inability of a person or organization to repay their debts.

Basis—the aggregation of productive forces and production relationships prevalent in a society.

Bond—a debt obligation stipulating repayment after a specific period of time and with a defined rate of interest.

Budget—a register of future income and expenses for a given period of time.

Capital—income-producing resources.

Credit—postponement of payment.

Default—failure of a state to repay its debts in full.

Deflation—insufficient amount of money and credit in circulation.

Denomination or face value—declared value of money or securities.

Emission—release of money or bonds into circulation.

Exchange—an organization that enables the orderly trade of shares, bonds, and any sort of standardized goods.

Exports—goods taken out of the country.

Hedging—additional transactions that reduce the risk of losses in the original transaction.

Imports—goods brought into a country.

Inflations—excessive amount of money and credit in circulation leading to price increases.

Interest—the cost of credit or postponement of payment.

Mode of production—combination of means of production and industrial relationship.

Money—means of exchanging goods and services, and making payments and savings.

Monopoly—a position so dominant in the market that it precludes competition.

Productive power—the means of production and people with their knowledge and skills that activate them.

Productive relationships—functional relationships among people who are involved in the process of production and distribution. The fundamental productive relationship is the ownership of the means of production and the goods and services produced.

Quotation—declared price.

Rate of exchange—the ratio at which one currency is exchanged for another.

Reexport—export of previously imported goods.

Securities—tradable financial assets.

Stock or share—a certificate that guarantees its owner a share in the profits of the issuing company.

Superstructure—the totality of the political, legal, and cultural framework of a society, including the predominant moral, aesthetic, and philosophical views.

www.ingramcontent.com/pod-product-compliance
Lightning Source LLC
Chambersburg PA
CBHW051321170526
45166CB00002B/637

* 9 7 8 1 4 7 8 7 5 4 8 0 0 *